# Understanding Social Engineering Based Scams

Markus Jakobsson

Editor

# Understanding Social Engineering Based Scams

 Springer

*Editor*
Markus Jakobsson
Agari

References to various copyrighted trademarks, servicemarks, marks and registered marks may appear in this book. Rather than use a trademark symbol with every occurrence of a trademarked name, logo, or image, this book uses the names, logos, and images only in an editorial fashion with no intention of infringement of the trademark.

ISBN 978-1-4939-8206-6        ISBN 978-1-4939-6457-4   (eBook)
DOI 10.1007/978-1-4939-6457-4

Printed on acid-free paper

This Springer imprint is published by Springer Nature
The registered company is Springer Science+Business Media LLC New York

*For A and Art*

# About the Editor and Contributors

**Dr. Markus Jakobsson** is a leading voice in advising on advancements in understanding phishing, crimeware, social engineering, and mobile security. He specializes in research around applied security, ranging from mobile malware detection to improved user interfaces, and with special attention to understanding and blocking fraud. Dr. Jakobsson has authored or co-authored more than a hundred peer-reviewed publications and numerous books related to Internet security and online fraud, including *Phishing and Countermeasures: Understanding the Increasing Problem of Electronic Identity Theft* (Wiley, 2006), *Crimeware: Understanding New Attacks and Defenses* (Symantec Press, 2008), *Towards Trustworthy Elections: New Directions in Electronic Voting* (Springer Verlag, 2010), *The Death of the Internet* (Wiley, 2012), and *Mobile Authentication: Problems and Solutions* (Springer Verlag, 2013). Dr. Jakobsson is the inventor of more than 100 patents and more than 100 pending patents, and consults as an expert witness in high-profile patent litigation cases. In 2013, Qualcomm acquired FatSkunk, an anti-malware startup founded by Dr. Jakobsson in 2009. He is the founder and CTO of ZapFraud, and Chief Scientist at Agari.

## Contributors

This book aims at giving a colorful and multifaceted view of emerging threats and countermeasures relating to social engineering and scams in general. The best way of assuring that a book like this represents many viewpoints is for the book to have many contributors, each one with his or her unique competence, insight, and passion. That is how this book was written.

The contributors, in alphabetical order, are Mayank Dhiman (Chap. 6), Ana Ferreira (Chap. 4), Sima Jafarikhah (Chap. 5), Markus Jakobsson (all chapters), Damon McCoy (Chaps. 2, 8, and 9), Youngsam Park (Chaps. 2, 8, and 9), Elaine Shi (Chaps. 2, 8, and 9), Hossein Siadati (Chap. 5), and Ting-Fang Yen (Chaps. 3, 6, and 10).

## Contributor Bios

**Mayank Dhiman** is a security researcher at Stealth Security Inc., a security startup. His primary interests include solving problems related to online fraud and Internet abuse. His current focus lies in detecting and mitigating malicious automation attacks. He is the co-author of several research papers and book chapters. Previously, he had stints at Facebook and PayPal where he worked on fraud- and abuse-related problems. He holds an MS in computer science from UC San Diego.

**Dr. Ana Ferreira** is a CISSP (Certified Information Systems Security Professional) and works as an IT specialist at the University of Porto, Portugal, since 2004. She has specialized in healthcare information systems access control, socio-technical aspects of security, and security usability, while she obtained an MSc in information security from Royal Holloway, University of London, in 2002 and a joint PhD in computer science in 2010 (University of Kent and University of Porto), and she has recently pursued a postdoctoral position at the University of Luxembourg. She is the author of 54 peer-reviewed conference and journal articles and three book chapters.

**Dr. Sima (Tahereh) Jafarikhah** received her PhD in 2013, specializing in theoretical computer science. More specifically, her work was concerned with different aspects of complexity and computability in analysis. She is currently associated with the computer science department at the City University of New York, doing research on cryptography, digital currencies, and computer security.

**Dr. Damon McCoy** is an assistant professor of computer science and engineering at New York University's Tandon School of Engineering. He received his PhD in computer science from the University of Colorado, Boulder. His research focuses on empirically measuring the security and privacy of technology systems and their intersections with society. Currently his primary focus is on online payment systems, economics of cybercrime, automotive systems, privacy-enhancing technologies, and censorship resistance.

**Dr. Youngsam Park**'s research focuses on understanding underground operation and economy of online scammers and cyber-criminals and seeking potential intervention points. His research interest includes empirical measurement of Nigerian scam and cybercrime. He received a PhD degree at the University of Maryland under the supervision of Dr. Elaine Shi and Dr. Damon McCoy and published papers on sales and rental scammers on Craigslist and DDoS-for-hire service.

**Dr. Elaine Shi** is an associate professor of computer science at Cornell University and a co-director of the Initiative for CryptoCurrencies and Contracts. Her research focuses on security and cryptography in general. Elaine obtained her PhD from Carnegie Mellon University. She is the recipient of a Packard Fellowship, a Sloan Fellowship, a VMWare Research Award, an NSA Best Scientific Cybersecurity Paper Award, and various other research awards and best paper awards.

**Hossein Siadati** is a PhD student at New York University where he researches end-user authentication, fraud, and social engineering problems and strives to provide practical solutions for them using psychology, data-analytic, and machine learning techniques. Mr. Siadati is co-author of several conference papers and book chapters.

**Dr. Ting-Fang Yen** is a research scientist at DataVisor, Inc. She specializes in security data analysis, with focus on the detection of online threats, including malware, malicious insiders and intrusions, and online fraud. Her research has shaped product directions and was published at top industry and academic security conferences. Dr. Yen received her MS and PhD degrees from Carnegie Mellon University and B.S. from National Chiao Tung University, Taiwan.

In addition, we have greatly benefitted from the kind feedback of many friends and colleagues. Linda Dobbs helped review the material and improve the flow. Timothy Bailey helped proofread the book. Bill Leddy, Aaron Emigh, and Chris Schille contributed technical insights. Arthur Jakobsson contributed to the understanding of how scammers are increasingly rather good at spelling. Jennifer Malat and Susan Lagerstrom-Fife, both from Springer, have helped answer questions and provide guidance.

# Contents

**Part V   Conclusion**

# An Overview of the Scam Problem

## About Scams and This Book

Email scams are almost as old as the Internet, but scammers were using regular mail long before there was email. The "Spanish Prisoner Letter" is believed to date back to the 1500. In this confidence game, the would-be victim receives a letter from a wealthy stranger, offering a handsome reward in exchange for a minor favor. While the principles of the scam have not changed much since the scam was first invented, the cost of delivering messages has come down dramatically, and with that, the prevalence of the scam has surged.

The low entry cost of doing business as a scammer, as well as the relative anonymity of the Internet, has given rise to a vast array of related ways for the scammer to convince the would-be victim to part with his or her money. Law enforcement is not a great impediment, as scammers often reside in countries where corruption is common. Moreover, these communities are typically not morally opposed to the idea of making wealthy foreigners subsidize local needs; successful scammers enjoy a certain Robin Hood stature and are seen as role models to underemployed segments of society. Given these favorable conditions and the relative absence of scam countermeasures, the scam problem has increased dramatically.

Until quite recently, email scams were typically easily detected by most people. Scams were characterized by poor grammar and spelling and commonly were based on rather outlandish storylines. In his 2002 paper titled "Why do Nigerian Scammers Say They Are from Nigeria?" [1], Cormac Herley of Microsoft analyzed why scammers intentionally tip off their victims, concluding that this common strategy does not repel the most gullible recipients, while the not-so-gullible would know not to respond. Therefore, this strategy helped the scammers "select" the recipients with the best benefit-cost ratio. This is a beneficial strategy when the only plausible victims are the very naïve (see, e.g., [2]) but not when the scams are credible to a wider audience.

As a result of a trend toward greater credibility, things have changed. Scammers have increasingly come to realize that by cleverly targeting their victims, rather than tipping them off, they can achieve even better returns. We can see the benefits of targeting in the context of phishing. Early phishing attacks were shotgun approaches. Studies of phishing (e.g., [3–5]) show that targeted phishing attacks can result in yields on the order of 75 %, which is more than an order of magnitude higher than un-targeted phishing attacks. As scammers have shifted their effort in the direction of increased targeting, they have also started to abandon the now less beneficial strategy of tipping off their victims. In general, their messaging has become more sophisticated. For example, 2008 was the year when scammers seem to have "learnt to spell." While security awareness campaigns still tell consumers to look out for poor grammar and spelling, this advice is no longer very meaningful, as sophisticated scammers now use language in much the same way as their intended victims.

Email scams have traditionally taken advantage of people's negative emotions, such as greed (e.g., in many 419 scams), loneliness (romance scams), and fear (security warnings, phishing, etc.). Recently, scammers have also started to impersonate mundane, legitimate business enquiries. For example, starting around 2010, scammers started targeting enterprises in scams commonly referred to as "business email compromise" (BEC) scams or "CEO fraud." In a BEC scam, the scammer skillfully impersonates a trusted entity, typically a colleague or vendor, asking the would-be victim to help perform a task. This task typically involves sending information or money. Scam emails of this type do not appeal to greed, loneliness, or fear; instead, they attempt to be as much "business as usual" as possible.

## About This Book

This book focuses on email scams, but many of the principles discussed apply equally to other delivery methods. (After all, the delivery method is largely inconsequential, and the approach the scammer takes is largely the same whether the come-on is delivered by email, instant message, or phone.) We describe recent trends and use insights about these both to gain a better understanding of scammers and their efforts and to help anticipate likely future developments. We describe the largely hopeless fight using *spam* filters against scammers and how scammers get around common filtering methods. We also describe how to implement various metrics, including methods for attack attribution, aimed at helping law enforcement identify and prosecute criminals. This book also views scams through the lens of case studies—ranging from how scammers find and target people using Craigslist to business email compromise scams and how to automate against these. The case studies provide details and insights related to scams and scammers. While the scammer methods described in the case studies are not used in *all* scams, they are representative of *many* scams. More importantly, they describe methods that can meaningfully measure and curb a large array of scam types, some of which may not even exist at the time this book is printed.

**How Will This Book Help You?** The book is written with a range of audiences in mind. If you are a network administrator, you are probably concerned with your users falling victim to scams, and you are looking for tools to help them avoid that—and techniques to identify likely problems. If you are a security researcher, this book may introduce you to some recent efforts into understanding social engineering and email scams in particular. If you are developing policy or best practices, then you need to know what techniques are meaningful and which ones are not. If you work in law enforcement, you are probably mostly interested in attack attribution and the collection of evidence. This book is written for all these people.

**What Does This Book Cover?** The book starts with an overview of the scam problem (Chap. 1). We then describe trends in scam—both from the perspective of historical trends (Chap. 2) and how to identify likely future trends based on user studies (Chap. 3). After reviewing trends, we turn to persuasion, addressing the question "What is persuasive, and why?" (Chap. 4). This lets us understand the underlying reasons driving the human part of the problem. In order to make full sense of trends, it is crucial to also understand the technical reasons for them. The most important aspect in this regard is probably what types of technologies are used to block the attempts of the scammers and how these technologies work—and the ways in which they do *not* work. This is reviewed in Chaps. 5 and 6, the latter of which gives an example of how content-based filtering could easily be circumvented. Chapter 7 then gives an example of a filter that was designed to address the shortcomings of existing content-based filtering and that was informed by an understanding of how scammers operate. At the heart of designing appropriate countermeasures against scams is the ability to measure the problem. Whereas it is possible to do this by analyzing reports and complaints, it is prudent to also attempt to measure things in real time—both to obtain faster answers and to avoid reporting bias among victims. Chapters 8, 9, and 10 describe how to design measurement studies that allow researchers and practitioners to understand what scammers do and to test countermeasures. It also describes methods for attack attribution, which is an important part of any law enforcement effort. This is followed in Chap. 11 by a deep dive into one type of scam that has recently surged dramatically—the business email compromise scam. The chapter looks at the reasons behind its success and describes common scammer strategies and how to design countermeasures based on an understanding of these strategies. In Chap. 12, we end the book with a conclusion and a list of important next steps.

**What Does This Book *Not* Cover?** This book does not attempt to be a comprehensive treatment of scams or even of email scams. It does not detail industry efforts such as DKIM and SPF, except by providing an overview of them and describing how these techniques are commonly circumvented. It also does not perform a deep dive into spam filtering technology—since such technologies are not very effective, because they are in constant flux, and because these approaches are already well documented and understood. The book does describe what techniques are in use, though, and the extent to which they address the problem of scams. This book is also not a comprehensive overview of scam countermeasures and scam research. Both of these are constantly changing to address how the threat changes.

**We Hope You Will Join the Fight.** This book offers an overview of trends and tools that the authors believe may be important to understand how to take the next few steps toward addressing this escalating threat. We hope that you, the reader, will be part of this effort—whether you are a practitioner, a researcher, or a policy maker. To fight this battle, we all need to work together.

Unquestionably, this book is not the last word in the battle between the scammers and the defenders against scams, and the staggering profits of the scammers will keep fueling the ingenuity of the scammers. On the other hand, this book aims to be a solid step in the direction of addressing the problem in a focused manner, based on measurements and a structural understanding. We hope you will build on the principles described in this book and will help curb the rising problem of scams before they do more damage to people, enterprises, and our ability to trust.

# References

1. C. Herley, Why do Nigerian Scammers say they are from Nigeria? in *Workshop on the Economics of Information Security (WEIS)* (2012)
2. M. Jacobs, Brother! Amazon Kindle Edition, ASIN: B0097C3H1Q (2012)
3. T.N. Jagatic, N.A. Johnson, M. Jakobsson, F. Menczer, Social phishing. Commun. ACM **50**(10), 94–100 (2007)
4. M. Jakobsson, S. Myers, *Phishing and Countermeasures: Understanding the Increasing Problem of Electronic Identity Theft* (Wiley-Interscience, New York, 2006)
5. M. Jakobsson, J. Ratkiewicz, Designing ethical phishing experiments: a study of (ROT13) rOnl query features, in *Proceedings of the 15th International Conference on World Wide Web* (ACM, 2006), pp. 513–522

# Chapter 1
# Scams and Targeting

**Abstract** This short chapter focuses on targeting. Targeting increases the yield of attacks, i.e., the response rate. Targeting also reduces the efficacy of spam filters and related technologies, and as such, vastly improves the profits scammers reap. We overview how to estimate the yield of attacks, and how to identify scams that are likely to become more common.

## 1.1 Yields and Targeting

Targeting a scam is known to dramatically increase the yield of the attack. Industry estimates of the yield of non-targeted phishing attacks fall in the range of a few percentage points, whereas targeted phishing attacks are believed to be an order of magnitude more effective. For example, in a 2011 report [1], Cisco details the economics of mass phishing attacks and targeted phishing attacks, as shown in Table 1.1. The table demonstrates how scammers benefit from targeting their victims. Here, the block rate is the likelihood with which the message gets blocked, e.g., by spam filters. The open rate is the probability that a recipient reads a delivered message. The click-through rate measures the probability that a user who reads the message clicks on a hyperlink in the message, and the conversion rate measures the likelihood that a recipient who clicks through falls for the attack by providing the information the attacker wants. As shown in Table 1.1, the probability that the recipient actually reads the message ("Open rate") is more than twenty times greater with targeted attacks. Even more importantly, the fraction of users who both read the message and click a hyperlink within it ("Click-through rate") is ten times higher with targeted attacks. The table suggests a tenfold increase in the profit of a campaign as a result of targeting, explaining why we see an increasing number of targeted attacks today.

However, the block rates suggested in the table are probably inaccurate. The difference between non-targeted and targeted attack block rates is likely to be much greater because the estimates in the table do not take into consideration the benefits that targeting scammers reap from circumventing spam filters. Remember that the

© Springer Science+Business Media New York 2016                    1
M. Jakobsson (ed.), *Understanding Social Engineering Based Scams*,
DOI 10.1007/978-1-4939-6457-4_1

**Table 1.1**  The economics of mass phishing vs. targeted phishing attacks

| Campaign type: | Mass phishing attack | Targeted phishing attack |
|---|---|---|
| Messages in campaign | 1,000,000 | 1,000 |
| Block rate | 99 % | 99 % |
| Open rate | 3 % | 70 % |
| Click-through rate | 5 % | 50 % |
| Conversion rate | 50 % | 50 % |
| Victims | 8 | 2 |
| Value per victim | $2,000 | $80,000 |
| Value per campaign | $16,000 | $160,000 |
| Cost of campaign | $2,000 | $10,000 |
| Profit from campaign | $14,000 | $150,000 |

block rate corresponds to the rate with which spam filters stop the delivery of the message. The Cisco report assumes this not to be affected by the quantity of messages being sent out. At high volumes, this is fairly accurate. However, as the volume drops, the block rate does too because many spam filters are based primarily on the reputation of the sender and on a velocity measure which corresponds to how many messages the sender transmits. When recipients place messages in the spam folder, the reputation of the sender goes down. Also, high velocity (i.e., large volumes of messages) causes messages to be classified as undesirable. This increases the rate of blocking. The Cisco estimates indicate a typical block rate of 99 % for 1,000 messages, corresponding to ten messages being received. However, by flying under the radar, the attacker can increase this number. By avoiding old email accounts with poor reputations, and by lowering the message quantity below the effective velocity threshold—perhaps as few as 100 messages per scam campaign—the attacker can make essentially *all* scam messages reach the victim.

If, as in our example, the block rate falls to zero for 100 messages (as it would for well-crafted messages that do not re-use low-reputation URLs, etc.), the number of victims increases by a factor ten compared to the example in the table.

## 1.2  Understanding Yields and Trends

Referring again to Table 1.1, the *yield* of an attack is the product of one minus the block rate, times the open rate, the click-through rate and the conversion rate. In the non-targeted example, the yield is therefore $(1 - 0.99) \times 0.03 \times 0.05 \times 0.50$, or a bit less than one in a million. The yield in the targeted attack can be computed as $(1 - 0.99) \times 0.70 \times 0.50 \times 0.50$, which is a bit less than one in five hundred—two thousand times higher.

The academic literature has examples of attacks with dramatically higher yields. For example, Jakobsson and Ratkiewicz [3] describe an experiment involving unwitting eBay users, in which the phishing attack had a yield of 11 %. This is more than sixty times higher than the yield in Table 1.1. Moreover, Jagatic et al. [2] carried out a study in which unwitting undergraduate students were sent carefully targeted phishing emails, supposedly aimed at stealing the login credentials for their university email accounts. In *that* study, a yield of 72 % was demonstrated. This is more than six times the yield of Jakobsson and Ratkiewicz, and 400 times higher than the yield of the targeted attack in the example used by Cisco.

If this leaves you confused, wondering who is right, here is the answer: they *all* are right. There is not *one* truth when it comes to what the yield of targeted attacks is—it simply depends on how well targeted the attack is, the context, the victim(s), and their preparedness. The insight to take home is therefore not the exact number, but the fact that targeting is tremendously profitable for scammers.

Clearly, the ability to target victims is of tremendous financial value to scammers. Doing so requires personal information about potential victims. One source of such information is the data stored by many large corporations. So, every time you see a news article lamenting another corporate breach, you should keep in mind what exactly fuels the breaches: the thirst for information about potential victims. Independently of the exact yield, it should be evident—by sheer market forces—that targeted attacks are here to stay, and will only increase.

# References

1. Email attacks: This time its personal. http://www.cisco.com/c/dam/en/us/products/collateral/security/email-security-appliance/targeted_attacks.pdf (2011)
2. T.N. Jagatic, N.A. Johnson, M. Jakobsson, F. Menczer, Social phishing. Commun. ACM **50**(10), 94–100 (2007)
3. M. Jakobsson, J. Ratkiewicz, Designing ethical phishing experiments: a study of (ROT13) rOnl query features, in *Proceedings of the 15th international conference on World Wide Web* (ACM, 2006), pp. 513–522

# Part I
# Identifying Trends

# Chapter 2
# Identifying Scams and Trends

**Abstract** This chapter focuses on the taxonomy of scam emails collected from various sources and investigates long-term trends in scam emails. We first describe a large-scale compendium of scam emails collected from various sources, and then present an analysis regarding what kind of scams exist, what their structures are, and how they are related to each other. We then describe a machine learning classifier built based upon the taxonomy analysis, and use it to cluster scam emails into major scam categories. Then an analysis of different trends from each scam category is presented. Our analysis shows a clear trend that spam-like *non-targeted scams* are decreasing continuously while *targeted scams* with specific victims have been getting more prevalent over the last 10 years.

## 2.1 Gathering Hundreds of Thousands of Scam Messages

To analyze the trends in scams, we collected extensive scam emails from several sources including scam reporting sites and a government report on internet crimes.

Scam emails collected from scam reporting sites, wherein anonymous users post scam emails they received, comprise the first data set. Amongst the many scam reporting sites, we selected four major ones with relatively large scam email databases, with more than thirty thousand scam emails in each site. We examined scam emails reported between 2006 and 2014, that is, more than ten thousand scam emails each year. Overall we collected about 220 thousand scam emails over the four scam reporting sites. Table 2.1 represents the summary of our scam email dataset.

A second source of scam data is the *FBI/IC3 annual reports* [3]. We refer to the FBI/IC3 annual reports to look at frequency of reporting and resulting financial loss to determine how harmful each type of scam has been.

## 2.2 Taxonomy of Scam Emails

In this section, scam email taxonomy is analyzed based on the scam email dataset described in Sect. 2.1. Since no de facto standard of scam categorization exists, the major scam categories frequently reported from users requires definition.

© Springer Science+Business Media New York 2016                                     7
M. Jakobsson (ed.), *Understanding Social Engineering Based Scams*,
DOI 10.1007/978-1-4939-6457-4_2

**Table 2.1**  Dataset summary

| Source | URL | Start date | End date | # Scam emails |
|---|---|---|---|---|
| Anti fraud international | Antifraudintl.org | 02/2007 | 12/2014 | 57,338 |
| Scam Warners | Scamwarners.com | 07/2008 | 12/2014 | 54,352 |
| Scamdex | Scamdex.com | 01/2006 | 12/2014 | 75,943 |
| 419baiter | 419baiter.com | 06/2008 | 02/2012 | 31,847 |
| Total | | | | 219,480 |

Summary of scam email dataset between 2006 and 2014

Although a few fraud taxonomies have been proposed [1, 3], and scam reporting sites have their own categorization rules, these classifications are not mutually consistent and do not cover all the types of scam present in our combined dataset. Also, each scam reporting site uses different scam categories. For example, the scam reporting site *anti fraud international* has twenty scam categories while the scam reporting sites *419baiter* and *scammed.by* do not categorize scam emails at all. Hence we built our own scam categorization as described in Table 2.1. Scam emails are categorized based on (1) whom scammers are pretending to be and (2) how scammers try to persuade their victims. Through the in-depth investigation of the collected scam emails and a survey of literature, we find ten scam categories (15 if counting subcategories) commonly used or frequently reported to the scam reporting sites. Table 2.2 gives a brief description of each of the 9 scam categories in our taxonomy of scam emails. This scam categorization result is used throughout Chap. 2.

### 2.2.1  Non-Targeted Scams

Our taxonomy of email scams first divides scams into three Types (see Table 2.2) depending on whether the email is *non-targeted*, *targeted* or *both*. A non-targeted scam is a traditional and typical form of email fraud where scammers do not set any designated victims; instead, like spammers, they send out as many scam emails as possible to anonymous users. A targeted scam aims at a specific victim based on a certain context (e.g., the victim is looking for a rent on Craigslist). Hence this type of scam can be more plausible. A few types of scam emails can be both non-targeted and targeted depending on the situation. For example, *Phishing* scam email can be delivered to many number of anonymous users just like spam emails, or it can be targeted on a specific victim based upon a context of the victim collected in advance.

- **Authority scams**: In *Authority scams*, scammers pretend to be employees at banks (*Bank scams*), government agencies or international organizations (*government/organization scams*). The scammers abusively use the names of renowned organizations (e.g., FBI and IMF) to gain trust of victims. In bank scams, scammers offers pre-loaded ATM cards or charity funds to victims,

**Table 2.2**  Scam email taxonomy

| Type | Category | Subcategory | Manual tagging | SVM classification |
|---|---|---|---|---|
| Non-targeted | Authority | Bank | 99 (5.0 %) | 18,680 (8.6 %) |
| | | Government, organization | 78 (3.9 %) | |
| | | Total | *177 (8.9 %)* | |
| | Loan | | 55 (2.8 %) | 6,428 (3.0 %) |
| | Lottery | | 215 (10.8 %) | 24,132 (11.1 %) |
| | Money transfer | Charity, dying person | 105 (5.3 %) | |
| | | Business, commodity | 185 (9.3 %) | |
| | | Next of kin | 367 (18.4 %) | |
| | | Widow, orphan, refugee | 118 (5.9 %) | 93,271 (42.8 %) |
| | | Etc. | 47 (2.4 %) | |
| | | Total | *822 (41.1 %)* | |
| Targeted | Business email compromise | | 54 (2.7 %) | 5,295 (2.4 %) |
| | Rental | | 43 (2.2 %) | 7,228 (3.3 %) |
| | Romance | | 203 (10.2 %) | 20,960 (9.6 %) |
| Both targeted and non-targeted | Employment | | 71 (3.6 %) | 10,191 (4.7 %) |
| | Sales | | 11 (0.6 %) | (Merged with business) |
| | Phishing | | 71 (3.6 %) | 9,368 (4.3 %) |
| Misc. | Others | | 165 (8.3 %) | |
| | Invalid emails | | 113 (5.7 %) | 22,192 (10.2 %) |
| | Total | | *278 (13.9 %)* | |
| Total | | | 2000 | 217,745 |

The ten most prevalent scam categories (excluding *Others* and *Invalid emails*), and the numbers (and percentage) of emails in our compendium belonging to each category based on manual tagging and an SVM classification

requiring a fee in advance. Similarly, scammers in government/organization scams notify their victims that they are able to receive charity funds and require a fee for the process. Sometimes these types of scams involve threats (e.g., unsolicited money related to an illegal business in the victim's account) or malware propagation (e.g., attachment containing virus or worms [4]). *Authority* scam emails mostly look like official emails from the organizations, and the processes explained in the emails also seem official.

- **Loan scams**: Scammers in *Loan scams* make a fake loan offer to victims at an attractive interest rate. But scammers ask for upfront fees for further loan service processing through money transfer companies such as Western Union or MoneyGram. Once a victim transfers the fee, scammers stop communicating with the victim.

- **Lottery scams**: *Lottery scams* bring the unexpected but happy news that the victim's email address has been entered into a lottery and has won the prize.[1] Scammers usually require a fee in advance for transferring a sum of prize money. This is one of the most typical and prevalent forms of non-targeted scams.
- **Money transfer scams**: Scammers in *Money Transfer scams* usually have funds in African countries and want to transfer the funds to victims' countries for several purposes. Scammers in *Charity/Dying Person scams* usually have an inheritance of several million in US dollars and ask victims to help move the money to a charitable fund in the victims' countries. *Business/commodity* scammers are looking for a business partner who will help them invest their money or sell their commodity in the victims' countries. The *Next of kin scam* is one of the most prevalent forms of fraud. Scammers in this category usually claim to be bankers or attorneys who have access to abandoned accounts of a client who has passed away. They propose putting the victim's name as a next of kin so that the victim can inherit the money. *Widow/orphan/refugee* scammers typically claim that they are in unstable countries suffering from internal wars or dictators. They have an inheritance from a parent or husband who has passed away recently and want to transfer the money out of their countries for safety. The *Etc.* subcategory includes scam emails that were not classified. In all cases, victims are promised a certain percentage of the transferred funds in return for helping the scammers, but the victims are also required to pay an upfront fee for the money transfer process.

## 2.2.2  Targeted Scams

In targeted scams, scammers may have obtained information about their potential victims, e.g., the fact that the victim is looking for an apartment on Craigslist or is selling an old iPhone on eBay. Since the scammers are able to exploit this knowledge, conversations in targeted scams are more natural and plausible.

- **Business email compromise scams**: *Business Email Compromise (BEC) scams* generally target specific companies that have dealings with foreign businesses. In this scam category, scammers can be sellers who present a product catalog with attractively priced goods or services, and sometimes they can be buyers who request a product list from victim businesses. Since scammers are "foreign" businesses, payments are usually done via wire transfer or other electronic payments. Seller scammers prefer these payment methods since they are easy to perform but hard to reverse. Likewise, buyer scammers also prefer them since it is relatively easy to fabricate fake payment notifications to victims.

---

[1]Oddly, to scammers, it is not *people* who are entered in lotteries, but *email addresses*. Correspondingly, email addresses, not their owners, are the winners of the lotteries.

- **Rental scams**: *Rental scams* may either target users who post listings on classified advertisements websites seeking a rental, or may post a fake rental listing by themselves to lure the victims. A common methodology of these scammers is to attract victims with low-priced rentals and then ask for an upfront fee for the first month rent and security deposit. The scammers often copy an actual rent listing and repost that with a much lower rent. They may ask the victims to inspect the house first, but usually a victim is not allowed to enter the house since the supposed home owner (scammer) is away for a good purpose (e.g., mission trip to African countries). Hence it may be hard for the victim to figure out if the rental listing is legitimate or not.
- **Romance scams**: *Romance scams* are slightly different from other types of scams in that scammers have to build a relationship with a victim over a relatively long time. Once the scammer successfully establishes a relationship with the victim, he may request money for various reasons, e.g., to purchase a airline ticket. Since the initial phase of a *Romance* scam is just "normal" conversation, it is relatively hard to determine whether it is scam. Please see Chap.10 for an in-depth study on *Romance* scams.

### 2.2.3 Scams that Are Both Non-targeted and Targeted

Certain types of scams fit both the non-targeted and targeted categories.

- **Employment scams**: *Employment* scams can be both non-targeted and targeted: non-targeted *Employment* scams, like spam, are sent to unspecified email addresses, and targeted *Employment* scams start with job listing on classified advertisements websites. One typical form of *Employment* scam starts with an attractive job offer from a company located outside of the victim's home country. Then the victim is usually required to provide an upfront fee for documentation process, e.g., visa application.
- **Phishing scams**: The general goal of *Phishing scams* is either to steal victim's private credentials (e.g., password or social security number) or to cause the victim to install malware by spoofing famous companies that hold the victim's money or account information (e.g., banks or PayPal). The key trick in this type of scam is links embedded inside emails that lead the victim to the scammer's own websites.
- **Sales scams**: In *Sales scams*, scammers can be either the seller or the buyer. The seller scammer posts a fraudulent ad on classified advertisements websites, and the buyer scammer responds to the victim's legitimate advertisement and makes a fake payment, e.g., a fake PayPal payment notification or a bogus check. One typical example of the *Sales* scam is the used car sales scam where a scammer posts a fraudulent ad selling a non-existent car on a classified advertisements website.

### 2.2.4  Miscellaneous Scams

In some cases, it is hard to classify a scam email into one of the scam categories listed in Table 2.2. Those scam emails are classified as *Miscellaneous* scams and not used in further analysis.

- **Others**: Scam emails that do not belong to any of the scam categories described above are classified as *Others* scams. Those are usually various scam categories with relatively low prevalence.
- **Invalid emails**: Some scam emails collected from scam reporting websites are not in valid form (e.g., no email content). These emails are classified as *Invalid emails*.

## 2.3  Scam Classification

Because the original source datasets do not provide a uniform, consistent email classification, we have classified each of the emails in our scam email dataset into the email scam categories described in the previous section.

The first step of scam classification is to establish the ground truth for the classification. Two thousand scam email samples randomly selected from our dataset were inspected manually and tagged on the scam categories listed in Table 2.2. The result of manual tagging is also shown in Table 2.2. The manual tagging result shows that about 41 % of all scam email samples are *Money transfer* scams. The second and third largest categories are *Lottery scams* and *Romance scams*, which account for about 11 and 10 % of scam email samples respectively. Both scam categories are also well-known, typical types of email scams.

A support vector machine (SVM) [2] classifier was implemented using the Python *scikit-learn* library [6] and was trained and evaluated using our 2,000 manually tagged scam email samples. Common English stop words (e.g., "a", "any", "am" and so on) and other non-alphabetical characters. (e.g., ":", "." and so on) were removed to eliminate meaningless terms from the feature space. Numerical characters and the dollar character "$" were retained since these are obviously meaningful. Term frequency–inverse document frequency (TF–IDF) [5] features were extracted from each sample and 80 % of the sample was randomly selected as the *training set* and 20 % as the *test set*. Then SVM classifier was trained based on the training set and its performance was evaluated using the test set. Evaluation of the SVM classifier was repeated ten times using different training and test sets, and the evaluation results are presented in terms of *precision/recall* and *ROC curves* in Fig. 2.1. To improve classification accuracy, scam emails were classified to the category level only. Additionally, *Business Email Compromise* scams and *Sales* scams were merged due to the similarity of email contents in such scams. The *Miscellaneous* scam category was not included in the SVM classifier evaluation since it accounts for a small number of various scam types.

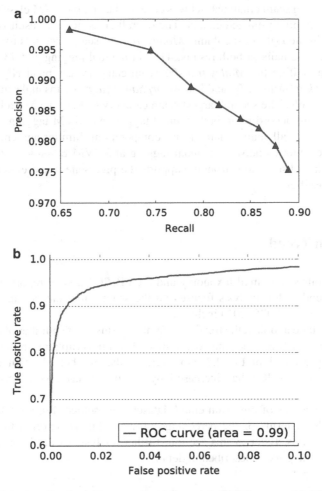

**Fig. 2.1** Precision/recall and receiver operating characteristic (ROC) curves of the SVM classifier. For ten major scam categories, the SVM classifier shows over 97 % precision with over 65 % recall, and the area under the ROC curve (AUC) is 0.99. All performance metrics are cross-validated averages measured using 2,000 samples divided randomly into training and test sets of size 80 and 20 %, averaged over ten repeats. (**a**) Precision/recall curve. (**b**) ROC curve

In Fig. 2.1a, the SVM classifier shows precision of higher than 97 % with at least 65 % recall for all scam categories. According to the receiver operating characteristic curve in Fig. 2.1b, the SVM classifier shows over 90 % true positive rate with lower than 1 % false positive rate. Although our SVM classifier may not show the minimal false positives and false negatives, it does demonstrate a sufficient performance to show overall trends in scams.

The remaining scam email dataset was classified using the SVM classifier trained on all of the manually-tagged emails. The overall classification result is presented in Table 2.2 in the rightmost column. *Money transfer* scam accounts for the largest portion of scam emails in both results, 41 % in manual tagging and 43 % in SVM classification. Within the *Money transfer* scam category, a typical Nigerian scam called *Next of kin* forms 18 %, and *Widow, orphan, refugee* scams make up about 6 % of all scam emails. The second largest scam category (other than Miscellaneous) is the *Lottery* scam according to both manual tagging and SVM tagging, accounting for about 11 % of all scam emails in our compendium. Similar agreement is seen in all scam categories between manual tagging and SVM classification results in Table 2.2. This observation strongly supports the preciseness and effectiveness of our SVM classifier.

## 2.4  Scam Trends

We can use our scam email taxonomy and the FBI/IC3 annual reports to examine long-term trends. Our analysis focuses on the scam email dataset and long-term trends for the years 2006–2014 inclusive.

First, let's take a look at the trends in scams in terms of the number of complaints made to the FBI/IC3. The annual number of scam complaints reported to the FBI/IC3 is presented in Fig. 2.2. On average, the number of scam complaints reported to the FBI/IC3 has increased by about 3 % each year between 2006 and 2014.

Now the analysis of our scam email dataset is presented. Figure 2.3 shows the overall trends in terms of the percentage of scam emails reported to four scam reporting websites. Later in this section, further analysis of the long-term trends of each scam category is described in detail.

### 2.4.1  Targeted vs. Non-Targeted Scams

Let's now consider the trend in how scam emails are targeted. Figure 2.4 shows the numbers of emails we classified as Targeted or Non-Targeted, respectively, in our compendium for the years 2006–2014. Scam categories belonging to "Both targeted and non-targeted" scams were excluded from the analysis to minimize confusion that may result from the ambiguous nature of the mixed scam categories. The analysis clearly shows that non-targeted scams have continuously decreased over the last 9 years while targeted scams have moved in the opposite direction.

In 2006, non-targeted scams accounted for the majority of scam emails (about 96 %) while targeted scams corresponded to a very limited percentage (about 1 %). In 2014, on the other hand, the percentage of non-targeted scams decreased drastically to 31 %, while targeted scams increased steeply to 48 %. This result

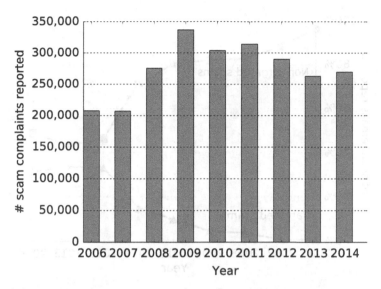

**Fig. 2.2** Number of scam complaints reported to the FBI/IC3 [3]. The number of scam complaints has increased on average by about 3 % each year

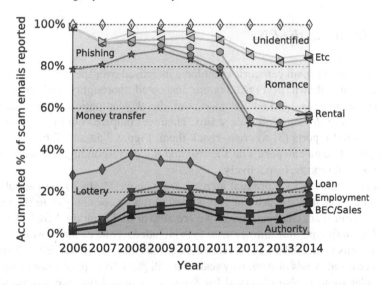

**Fig. 2.3** Fraction of scam emails reported to scam reporting websites

implies that scammers' fraud methodology has improved, from simple spam-like scams (e.g., *Lottery* and *Money transfer* scams) to more personalized and plausible scams aided information about specific victims (e.g., *Business email compromise*, *Romance* and *Sales* scams).

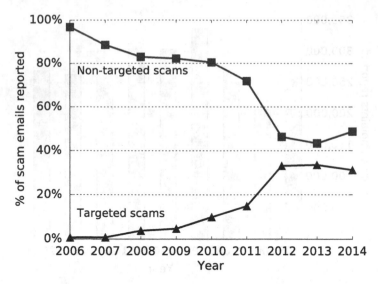

**Fig. 2.4** Targeted vs. non-targeted scams. Targeted scams increase continuously from 1 % in 2006 to 31 % in 2014, but non-targeted scams decrease from 96 % in 2006 to 48 % in 2014

## 2.4.2  Scams on the Rise

Now let us present scam categories that have increased over the years. The overall trends in scam shown in Fig. 2.3 were inspected thoroughly and three scam categories showing a marked increase over the 9 year period were identified: *Authority, BEC/Sales* and *Romance* scams. Then we compared our findings with the FBI/IC3 annual reports [3] to cross-check them. Figure 2.5a and Table 2.3 shows the analysis of scam categories on the rise and the corresponding results from the FBI/IC3 annual reports, respectively.

*Authority* scams show a gradual increase from about 2 % in 2006 to about 13 % in 2010 and 12 % in 2014. Although it is hard to match our analysis to the reports due to different scam categorizations, we are able to find from the FBI/IC3 reports that *FBI scam* (a type of *Authority* scams) is included as one of the most frequently reported scams from 2009 to 2014. Even though the *FBI* scam in the FBI/IC3 reports does not cover all kinds of *Authority* scams, it still partially supports our analysis.

A similar trend is also observed for *Romance scams*. Romance scams show a rapid increase from less than 1 % in 2006 to 20 % in 2012. According to the FBI/IC3 reports, the Romance scam also has been prevalent from 2011 and is included in the most frequently reported scams.

*BEC/Sales* scams also increase continuously over the 9 years, from about 1 % in 2006 to about 3 % in 2014, both as a fraction of the entire volume of self-reported scam emails. Although neither *BEC* or *Sales* scams were identified as one of the most frequently reported scams in the FBI/IC3 annual reports, *BEC* scam is now considered an emerging scam category. According to the 2014 FBI/IC3

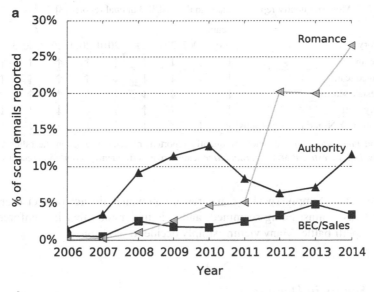

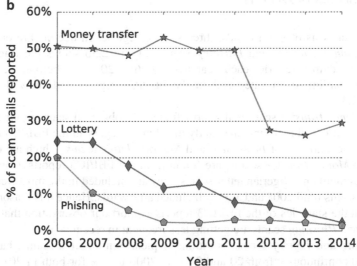

**Fig. 2.5** Trends in scams. Fraction of all emails classified into scam categories on the rise (*panel a*) and in decline (*panel b*). (**a**) Scams on the rise. (**b**) Scams in decline

annual report, the *Business Email Compromise* (BEC) scam was first reported in 2010 and has evolved into more sophisticated and various forms since 2013. Since January 2015, the FBI has seen a 270 % increase in identified victims and exposed loss, with reported losses exceeding $2.3 billion in losses between late 2013 and early 2016. It should be understood that the entire scam problem is likely to be under-reported, though, since since most victims recognize that there is likely to

**Table 2.3** Most frequently reported scams in the FBI/IC3 annual reports [3]

| Category | Years | | | | | | | | |
|---|---|---|---|---|---|---|---|---|---|
| | 2006 | 2007 | 2008 | 2009 | 2010 | 2011 | 2012 | 2013 | 2014 |
| FBI scams | ↓ | ↓ | ↓ | ↑ | ↑ | ↑ | ↑ | ↑ | ↑ |
| Romance scams | ↓ | ↓ | ↓ | ↓ | ↓ | ↑ | ↑ | ↑ | ↑ |
| Real estate scams | ↓ | ↓ | ↓ | ↓ | ↓ | ↓ | ↑ | ↑ | ↑ |
| Identity theft | ↑ | ↑ | ↑ | ↑ | ↑ | ↓ | ↓ | ↓ | ↓ |
| Investment & Nigerian letter scams | ↑ | ↑ | ↑ | ↓ | ↓ | ↓ | ↓ | ↓ | ↓ |

*FBI* and *Romance* scams are more frequently reported in recent years. On the other hand, *Identity theft*, *Investment* and *Nigerian letter* scams are less frequently reported in recent years

be no recourse. Simply speaking, insurance companies do not protect users and organizations against being scammed, and it is understood that law enforcement fights an uphill battle. Many victims simply decide to move on.

## 2.4.3 Scams in Decline

From the analysis of scam trends, three scam categories in decline are observed: *Lottery, Money transfer* and *Phishing* scams. Figure 2.5b shows the fraction of those three scam categories each year from 2006 to 2014. As before, we looked for corresponding scam categories in the FBI/IC3 reports and show the result in Table 2.3.

The *Money transfer* scam is the most frequently observed scam in our dataset, but it was not possible to find an exactly matching category in the FBI/IC3 reports. However the statistics of *Investment* and *Nigerian letter scams*, which are directly related to *Money transfer* scams, are found from the FBI/IC3 reports. Combining both investment and Nigerian letter scams, they are included in the most frequently reported scams until 2008 and are not included afterwards. Hence it is reasonable to argue that the statistics of the FBI/IC3 reports support our observation that *Money transfer* and *Phishing* scams are getting less frequent in recent years.

*Phishing* and *Lottery* scams, additional typical non-targeted scams, have also decreased continuously from 20 and 24 % in 2006 to 3 % for both in 2014. Even though it was not possible to find an exact match, the statistics of *Identity theft*, which is a close match to *Phishing* scam, was found in the FBI/IC3 reports. As shown in Table 2.3, identity theft was one of the most frequently reported scams until 2010 and was not included afterwards.

# References

1. M. Beals, M. DeLiema, M. Deevy, Framework for a taxonomy of fraud. http://fraudresearchcenter.org/wp-content/uploads/2015/07/FFRC_Taxonomy_FullReport_7-22-15.pdf (2015)
2. C. Cortes, V. Vapnik, Support-vector networks. Mach. Learn. **20**(3), 273–297 (1995)
3. Federal Bureau of Investigation, Internet Crime Complaint Center (IC3) annual reports. https://www.ic3.gov/media/annualreports.aspx
4. M. Jakobsson, Z. Ramzan, *Crimeware: Understanding New Attacks and Defenses*, 1st edn. (Addison-Wesley Professional, Indianapolis, 2008)
5. K.S. Jones, A statistical interpretation of term specificity and its application in retrieval. J. Doc. **28**(1), 11–21 (1972)
6. F. Pedregosa, G. Varoquaux, A. Gramfort, V. Michel, B. Thirion, O. Grisel, M. Blondel, P. Prettenhofer, R. Weiss, V. Dubourg, J. Vanderplas, A. Passos, D. Cournapeau, M. Brucher, M. Perrot, E. Duchesnay, Scikit-learn: machine learning in Python. J. Mach. Learn. Res. **12**, 2825–2830 (2011)

# Chapter 3
# Predicting Trends

**Abstract** Being able to identify likely trends is the core of building better countermeasures. This chapter describes a light-weight approach to identifying differences in user vulnerabilities. That allows us to quantify vulnerabilities before they are actively abused. By being able to anticipate what fraudsters will be likely to do eventually, it is possible to build countermeasures that address big open vulnerabilities.

## 3.1  Vulnerabilities Point to Trends

Unexploited vulnerabilities do not always get noticed by attackers, but it is safe to assume that the greater the vulnerability is, the sooner attackers will start taking advantage of it. The reason is simple: whereas fraudsters do not always intuitively pick the highest yielding attack right away, they are keenly aware of how well each effort works. Therefore, they see both when a new variant fails to work and when a new version works above and beyond expectations.

In the context of scams, the success can be thought of as the product of the persuasiveness of a scam message and the failure rate of existing countermeasures. The persuasiveness therefore corresponds to the yield of the attack in the absence of countermeasures. To determine what types of attacks may increase in importance and so accordingly focus the development of counter-measures, this relationship must be understood.

Whereas fraud researchers have studied the yield of potential attacks for years, these studies are often very involved and time consuming. These studies mimic an entire attack: the selection of the "victims"; what information is used to convince the victims; and how the messaging is done, down to what images and what fonts are used. Therefore, they result only in an insight into how well one pitch would work for one audience. If the studies are performed at universities, they require approval from Internal Review Boards (see, e.g., [3] for an overview of the complexities and importance of IRB review). As a result, researchers find it difficult to rapidly study many related versions of a problem or to make modifications to studies. The need to

© Springer Science+Business Media New York 2016
M. Jakobsson (ed.), *Understanding Social Engineering Based Scams*,
DOI 10.1007/978-1-4939-6457-4_3

try different pitches and different targeting approaches would significantly increase the costs of such efforts and the time to perform the studies. To address this problem and create a more nimble experimental approach, a modular approach has been developed [2] in which the problem is broken down into its components. This allows the researcher to identify what pitch works the best without having to worry about the targeting, and vice versa.

Simply put, one can argue that the persuasiveness of a scam message is the product of the credibility of the message and how well targeted it is. Imagine, for example, that a person manages to convince everybody in an audience of a hundred to give him all their change (a 100 % credible pitch), but only half of the people have any change (a 50 % targeting of the message). In this example, the persuasiveness, measured from the outcome of the effort, is 50 %. The same result, of course, would be obtained from somebody who manages to convince only half of an audience of a hundred people, but where everybody in the audience had change in their pockets.

## 3.2   Measuring Credibility

We will now describe an approach to quantify the probability that typical recipients find scam emails credible.

First of all, let's talk about what *cannot* be done. You cannot ask people "Is *this* credible?," while showing them an email or a website. The reason is that this question will, unquestionably, make people unusually suspicious that something is amiss and they will scrutinize the email or website more carefully than ever. Then you are not measuring the likely reaction of users, but their maximum abilities [1]. This may also be interesting, but not if you care about anticipating what people will fall for or what types of scams will become more common.

What you *can* do is to ask a collection of subjects to review one or more emails and websites, and assess the credibility of these emails by asking the subjects to indicate the nature of the primary risk associated with each [2]. One option would be the *actual* risk, if any; some options may correspond to other, plausible risks; and yet others to risks that are not realistic, or which are not significant in light of the actual risk. By asking people to identify the *primary* risk from a collection of possibilities of varying degrees of correctness, you can detect the portion of the test takers whose selection would place them at risk for failing to understand what the *real* risk was. Remember that it does not matter what one or two subjects think. You want to treat the subjects as statistical entities, and determine what "people in general" would think. You need hundreds of subjects. Then you can determine, statistically speaking, what people find credible.

Let's look at an example. Assume we want to measure the likely yield of two potential phishing attacks with slightly different messaging. The first attack may be the phishing attack shown in Fig. 3.1, in which the recipient is told that his or her email quota is insufficient, and the second is the "take a survey" phishing

1. Assume you received an email like the following email. What type of risk is this <u>primarily</u> associated with?

**ACCOUNT NOTICE: ACTION REQUIRED:**
**You have exceeded your mailbox quota. Your account will be blocked 8 AM tomorrow unless you request more space. You can request more space by clicking <u>here</u>.**

○ The recipient may get a computer virus.

○ The recipient may lose her password.

○ This may be a scam aimed at stealing your money.

○ There is no risk.

○ The recipient may get unwanted advertisements.

○ The recipient's account may be blocked if she does not pay attention.

**Fig. 3.1** Assessing message credibility. The figure shows a phishing email that is commonly used by scammers to gain a foothold in a targeted enterprise by gaining access to the email account of a user

2. Assume a person named George received the following email soon after purchasing a pair of shoes on Amazon. What type of risk is this <u>primarily</u> associated with?

**Prime Code #ec61ec5e-0af9-42cf-9201-95cad0edd260**

**Hello George!**

**Thank you for your recent Amazon purchase. Our mission is to improve customer service. Therefore, we would like to ask for your feedback on your recent purchase experience. Please answer three yes/no questions and claim your $25 card to use as you please.**

<u>**Click to answer the survey and claim your gift card.**</u>
**Redeem by: April 25, 2015**

**Thank you for taking the time to improve your experience. Please visit us again soon.**

○ There is no risk.

○ The recipient may get a computer virus.

○ The recipient may lose her password.

○ The gift card may expire very soon.

○ The recipient may be cheated and not receive a gift card after answering the survey.

○ This may be a scam aimed at stealing your money.

**Fig. 3.2** Assessing message credibility. The figure shows a new variant of a scam that has existed for more than 10 years, in which the recipient is asked to respond to a survey in return for a financial award. To receive the award, the user has to enter personal information, including her password and bank account information, on a site he/she believes is associated with the surveying organization

attack shown in Fig. 3.2. Say that we wish to know which pitch is likely to be most successful. We will describe the "modular" approach to determining the likely yield of each of the variants. This is based on asking a sufficiently large number of "test takers" what the primary risk associated with the email is—preferably for a large number of emails, some of which are not risky at all—where the subjects select the primary risk from a list. See Fig. 3.1 for the first list of potential answers that the subject can choose from.

The correct answer in Fig. 3.1 is "The recipient may lose her password", as typically, a victim of this type of scam is asked to sign in to what he or she is made to believe is his or her email service provider. However, since the email has a clickable link, the answer "The recipient may get a computer virus" (40 %) is also a reasonable response. A user who responds this way does not have a deep knowledge of scams, but still identifies this risk as a possibility. The answer is *reasonable* in that it causes a respondent selecting this answer to react in a similar way as a respondent who selects the *correct* answer. Similarly, the response "This may be a scam aimed at stealing your money" (19 %) is reasonable, since the end goal of the scammer may be to do so. On the other hand, the responses "There is no risk" (3 %), "The recipient may get unwanted advertisements" (5 %) and "The recipient's account may be blocked if she does not pay attention" (23 %) are naive. The credibility of this message can therefore be said to be 31 %, or put another way, 31 % of the respondents would find the message sufficiently credible that he or she would be at risk.

In the past, the attack shown in Fig. 3.2 has not used any targeting, but recently, it has been seen to target (and correctly name) Amazon Prime members—including accounts used uniquely for Amazon purchases. This suggests a potential breach or misbehavior of at least one Amazon seller. The "prime code" in the body of the scam message is likely to be used to circumvent spam filters based on message digests—different batches of the scam will use different codes here.

The correct answer in Fig. 3.2 is "The recipient may lose her password" (8 %). The reasonable answers are "The recipient may get a computer virus "(15 %) and "This may be a scam aimed at stealing your money" (24 %). The naive answers are "There is no risk" (13 %); "The gift card may expire very soon" (7 %); and "The recipient may be cheated and not receive a gift card after answering the survey" (33 %). In total, 53 % of the respondents therefore find this message credible. Therefore, by performing two quick surveys, one can determine that the second attack is likely to be substantially more effective than the first one, but that they are both very credible. "Traditional" phishing attacks in which a user gets an email from a bank requiring him or her to log in have single-digit yields.

To avoid biasing test takers, it is beneficial to add non-scam messages to the survey. See Fig. 3.3 for an example. Also, randomizing the order of the questions is helpful.

While a modular approach is very helpful to identify likely user vulnerabilities, not all questions can be answered in this way. Chapters 8–10 give examples of situations that cannot be addressed using this experimental method—along with descriptions of how to do it instead.

**5.** Assume you received the following email. What type of risk is this <u>primarily</u> associated with?

**The Dish**
-------------------
**Ellen Degeneres and Portia De Rossi may be having their fair share of problems....**
**But is plastic surgery really the answer??**

**Did Ellen get a facelift to get Portia to stay with her?**
**We can't show you the pics that started the rumors but we can show you what Ellen did:**
<u>Check it out.</u>

**We think that Ellen learned from horror shows like Meg Ryan and Nicole Kidman...**
**Here's what she really did to turn back the clock 20 yrs -> click <u>here</u>.**

○ This may cause you to get a computer virus.

○ The sender may want you to have plastic surgery.

○ The sender may want to steal your credit card information.

○ There is no risk.

○ The sender may provide you with false news.

○ This may be a scam aimed at stealing your money.

**Fig. 3.3** Assessing message credibility. This question was added as a red herring. It is spam rather than scam. Whereas there may be risks associated with malware infection, for example, this was simply added to make the respondents not focus too much on concerns with phishing. The responses were ignored by the authors of the study since this was not what they were focusing on

# References

1. V. Anandpara, A. Dingman, M. Jakobsson, D. Liu, H. Roinestad, Phishing IQ tests measure fear, not ability, in *Proceedings of 11th International Conference on Financial Cryptography and Data Security* (2007), pp. 362–366
2. M. Jakobsson, T.-F. Yen, How vulnerable are we to scams? in *BlackHat* (2015)
3. M. Jakobsson, N. Johnson, P. Finn, Why and how to perform fraud experiments. IEEE Secur. Priv. **6**(2), 66–68 (2008)

# Part II
# Why Do People Fall for Scams?

# Chapter 4
# Persuasion in Scams

**Abstract** This chapter identifies and analyzes trends in the terms and expressions used in the content of scam emails and associates those with the principles of human persuasion that they integrate. We discuss and compare both the terms and principles used over time within a sample of scam emails collected between 2006 and 2014. Our analyses shows that different scam email categories use various principles of persuasion and that it is possible to observe distinct trends in their usage. We argue that with a better understanding of how scammers work at a psychological level, one could devise new techniques to detect persuasion in scam emails and build tools that more closely emulate human interaction with those emails.

## 4.1 Persuasion in Emails

Persuasion has always been part of human interaction. It can be used to influence and support good or improved behavior [13], but it can also be used to trick and manipulate people into performing actions that can end in some kind of loss (e.g., divulging confidential information [16] or giving money to fraudsters.)

Within the field of information security, the art of using human skills and persuasion techniques to obtain unauthorized information is called social engineering. One very common conduit for social engineering is email. Scam and phishing emails can be highly disruptive to organizations as they have the potential to mislead key personnel in order to gain access to a myriad of sensitive services and data. Human Resources, Accounting and Finance are the departments within an organization that deal with personal and financial data. Because the Human Resources skill set includes a high level of employee interaction and comprehensive personnel skills and capacity assessment, it is reasonable to expect that Human Resources workers would be better than their colleagues in recognizing phishing emails. Similarly, Accounting and Finance personnel, with their conversance of employee's salaries and organizational expenses, would be expected to be more careful than the average employee in guarding a company's financial information. Unfortunately this is not always the case [14].

In addition, in today's highly connected society, even if these employees were technically savvy, their IT literacy might not be enough to prevent them from falling for scams. As an individual spends more time on the Internet or communicating by

© Springer Science+Business Media New York 2016    29
M. Jakobsson (ed.), *Understanding Social Engineering Based Scams*,
DOI 10.1007/978-1-4939-6457-4_4

email [2, 9], the brain creates routines, which can help deal with and process things more efficiently. But these routines can also compromise the ability to pay attention and to cause the brain to bypass details within the message which would help detect fraudulent content, increasing the likelihood of clicking on a dishonest or scammy link [11].

So what about all the effort and research that has been put into making scam filters more proficient at detecting scam emails? Most scam filters use techniques to identify email keywords, grammatical inconsistencies, typos or information misplacement [1, 5, 12, 17]. These can help scam filters to have a wider range of detection but can also provide for many false positives since typos and inconsistencies are also frequent in legitimate human-written emails while with automatically generated emails, it may depend if the used template has mistakes or not. Many non-automated methods focus on educating users to identify scam and phishing emails [12]. These can be through online games or cue messages that help the user to recognize fake email messages. However, the aforementioned methods (i.e., scam filtering and education) are effective only against the types of scam messages for which they were designed. Scammers are continuously changing the content of their emails to defeat these approaches, and their new content will not be recognized until the new signature is integrated within the filtering mechanisms. Thus, these prevention methods tend always to be one step behind the scammers.

To address this problem, means are needed to widen the identification of scam emails through scrutinizing the persuasive content rather than just evaluating the form and structure. One approach to persuasion used by scammers involves the use of meaningful contextual information such as victims' online shopping or banking preferences [10], to make scam emails seem more appealing and trustworthy. In addition, a plethora of other persuasive elements—logos, graphics, colors, or words and phrases that are recognizable by the recipients—can be employed to make dishonest emails appear legitimate and even personal [7]. All these components can heighten the social presence of a scam email and alter the recipients' cognitive processes to provoke a sense that s/he is corresponding with a real, trustworthy and even known person [7].

Social engineers know that to influence and persuade more efficiently they have not only to inform people but also to link their message to deep human motivations. By identifying principles of influence within scam messages, we are able to understand why these principles are so successful and study more innovative ways to tackle those messages.

## 4.2 Principles of Persuasion

We list now the principles of persuasion that are used in scam messages and were defined in [4].

- AUTHORITY: Society trains people not to challenge authority but to respond to it without questioning. People usually follow an expert or a figure of authority and will do a great deal for someone they think is in charge.

  *Examples of ways the authority principle can be used*: (a) someone pretending to be a doctor by using a white coat in a hospital. This person can access restricted areas, confidential and sensitive patient records and even pretend to treat patients, thereby putting their privacy and their lives in danger; or (b) a scam email, purporting to be from the victim's bank and including the bank's logo, urgently requiring the client to update personal and bank details. The email includes bold and red text to stress the urgency of the message and threatens to block the account soon if the client does not take the required action.

- SOCIAL PROOF: People tend to mimic what the majority of people around do or seem to be doing, so they let their guard and suspicion down and prefer to share the same responsibility and risks. It is easier (and probably safer) to follow the consensus of a group, even if it may be wrong, than to follow the opinion or behavior of one person that is acting opposite to everybody else.

  *Examples of ways the social proof principle can persuade include*: (a) in a gambling situation, other people playing the game seem to be winning (but they are part of the fraud) or the game does not look so hard to win. The victim may be tempted to bet and engage in the game, which then suddenly becomes much harder to win; or (b) a scam email from an alleged system administrator with an email address of the company where the recipient works asking them to test a link that supposedly takes the user to his/her mailbox. The sender knows the recipient's email address and that s/he works in that specific company.

- LIKING, SIMILARITY & DECEPTION: People prefer to follow or relate to other people whom they know, like, are attracted to, or who seem familiar or similar to themselves.

  *Examples of the liking, similarity & deception principle can include*: (a) good-looking political candidates that will have more votes, or sellers that appear to have similar behavior and tastes to a person will be more successful in selling to that person; or (b) a scam email from a supposed friend of the recipient asking him/her to visit a website that is really interesting.

- COMMITMENT, RECIPROCATION & CONSISTENCY: People feel more confident in their decision once they commit (publicly) to a specific action and need to follow it until the end. This type of persuasion often also leverages people's need to appear consistent and believe in reciprocity for instance, when they owe a favor. Reciprocating a favor or responding to some action can be an automatic response that is linked to some previous commitment or consistent with a previous situation.

  *Examples of commitment, reciprocation & consistency persuasion are*: (a) when someone gives you a flower or a pin in exchange for money for the poor, although it may seem to be a sales' transaction, it is implicitly considered as a protocol where people are bound to reciprocate somehow either by repaying a favor or carrying on with the transaction; or (b) a scam email where the sender knows beforehand that the recipient is looking to buy a house and sends an email with a fraudulent ad which promises a very good price for a house with the same characteristics and on the same location the recipient has been lately looking for. In order to secure it, the recipient needs to urgently pay for a deposit. The principle is expressed in the fact that the victim has previously searched for similar houses (consistency) and in order to get this great deal needs to reciprocate (carry on the transaction) with a security deposit so to commit to buy it later.

- DISTRACTION: People's tendency to get distracted can also be leveraged to persuade. When people focus on one thing, they can ignore other things that may happen. They may focus attention on what they can gain, lose, or need, or on whether an item will be soon unavailable, has been censored or restricted, or will be more expensive later. These distractions can heighten people's emotional state and make them forget other important considerations when making decisions.

    *Distraction plays a key role when*: (a) someone buys a toy to offer his/her child because it is said to become unavailable soon. Parents may be forced to buy the toy at that moment since the child has been pressing a lot for it, and do not take some time to verify whether that toy is that rare in other shops or even on the Internet; or (b) a scam email to acknowledge that the recipient has won a substantial lottery prize, since the victim's focus is directed to how s/he can have access to the money. This diverts attention from other details of the email that otherwise might give it away as a scam (i.e, the recipient does not know the sender as a legitimate lottery site or s/he has not bought a ticket in years) and prevents the recipient from reasoning about the message's authenticity.

Having reviewed these principles, we are now ready to consider how they are commonly used in various types of scams illustrated by examples from recent scam email messages. (For the reader interested in more details about the principles, we refer to Cialdini et al. [3] as well as other authors [6, 18].)

## 4.2.1  Principles of Persuasion in Scam Categories

Here we present the association between scam email categories that were introduced in Sect. 2.2, and the principles of persuasion, according to their descriptions and goals (Tables 4.1 and 4.2).[1] With this information, we can identify what principles of persuasion are commonly used in the various types of scam emails in the analyzed sample. Scam email categories can be targeted (e.g., addressed to a specific recipient and can also include information on his/her personal interests), non-target (e.g., general and not addressed to a specific recipient) and a mixture of both depending on the degree of customization each email may contain (e.g., Sales and Employment categories in Table 4.2).

---

[1]Principles that are named by the merging of several other names refer to one principle that is represented with the concatenation of various names using a '+'.

**Table 4.1**  Persuasion principles used in non-targeted scams

| Scam category | Scam description | Principle(s) in category | Principle's description |
|---|---|---|---|
| Authority | – Sender requires a fee<br>– Sender pretends to work for Government/Company<br>– It may involve a threat | Authority | Not to question authority and follow or respond quickly to an expert or pretense of authority |
| Loan<br><br><br>Lottery | – Sender requires a fee in exchange of a loan service<br><br>– Sender requires a fee to provide a winning prize | Commitment+ Reciprocation+ Consistency & Distraction & Authority | Recipient feels obliged to respond to a request that may end in loss by focusing on what can be gained instead, so not checking for the email's legitimacy |
| Money Transfer | – Recipient receives a donation<br>– Sender asks a contribution to help others<br>– Sender proposes a business offer<br>– Recipient receives an inheritance from strangers<br>– Sender asks for a fee to transfer money | Commitment+ Reciprocation+ Consistency & Distraction | Recipient may have the urge to help or focuses on what can be gained by responding to the email, so avoiding closer inspection to its legitimacy |
| Phishing | – Spoofing companies that hold victim's personal details or money | Liking+ Similarity+ Deception | Sender pretends to be familiar or known to the victim |

The table links each non-targeted scam email category and shows which principles of persuasion are utilized by each category.

Not surprisingly, the Authority scam category uses the principle of persuasion also named *Authority*. This type of scam messages usually come from a figure with power or reputation who requests from the victim an urgent action such as a reply to a message. The message may even include a threat to block or limit some service that is possibly connected to the victim. This category of scam emails is increasing (Fig. 2.5 in Chap. 2) so scammers frequently focus on the use of the *Authority* principle to obtain more successful replies. Authority or pretense of authority is an effective way to influence because society has conditioned us to obey to whomever seems to be responsible in a certain context, in this case, a bank, government or a major organization.

Figure 4.1 shows an example of an Authority scam email using the principle of Authority. This is a traditional but still popular phishing scam. The email seems to originate from Paypal, according to its logo, and instructs the recipient to click on a button to update his/her billing information. It includes further elements that urge the recipient either to obey the request or risk losing the service. Commonly, this type of scam message, with all elements of the email making sense and in the right place, induces an automatic propensity to reply as soon as possible, without even questioning the message's legitimacy. Additionally, because these scam emails

**Table 4.2** Principles of persuasion used in scams

| Scam category | Scam description | Principle(s) in category | Principle's description |
|---|---|---|---|
| Business Email Compromise scams | – Sender presents product catalog with attractive prices<br>– Sender interested in buying from the recipient | Commitment+ Reciprocation+ Consistency & Distraction | Recipient is interested in a good deal or improving his/her sales' goals so persuaded to reply to the scam email. Plus s/he will focus on what can be gained by answering the email, so avoiding closer inspection to its legitimacy |
| Rental | – Recipient gets a fraudulent advantageous rental ad<br>– Sender asks for a security deposit/month in advance | Commitment+ Reciprocation+ Consistency & Distraction | Recipient feels obliged to repay a favor or is asked to commit to a certain action. Plus s/he will focus on what can be gained by answering the email, so avoiding closer inspection to its legitimacy |
| Romance | – Sender builds a relationship with the victim to ask him/her for money later | Liking+ Similarity+ Deception & Commitment+ Reciprocation+ Consistency & Distraction | Sender pretends to be familiar and known to the victim and make recipient help someone s/he knows and/or likes |
| Sales | – Recipient gets a fraudulent ad or receives a fake payment | Commitment+ Reciprocation+ Consistency & Distraction | Recipient feels obliged to repay a favor and will focus on what can be gained by answering the email, so avoiding closer inspection to its legitimacy |
| Employment | – Sender requires a fee in exchange of documentation | Commitment+ Reciprocation+ Consistency & Distraction & Authority | Recipient feels obliged to respond to a request that may end in loss by focusing on what can be gained instead, so not checking for the email's legitimacy |

The table shows which principles of persuasion are utilized by scams in the (Business email compromise, Rental and Romance) and targeted/non-targeted (Sales and Employment) categories

target clients of the purported well-known sender, the recipient has a much higher probability of believing the email is from a legitimate source.

Figure 4.2 describes another example within the Bank scam email subcategory that uses the Authority principle. To impersonate a known authority, a real logo is used together with detailed meaningful and contextualized information regarding the alteration of services. An imminent deadline is set, after which the recipient will be unable to access services as previously. To preserve access, the recipient needs to perform specific actions mandated by the email. Again, all elements seem

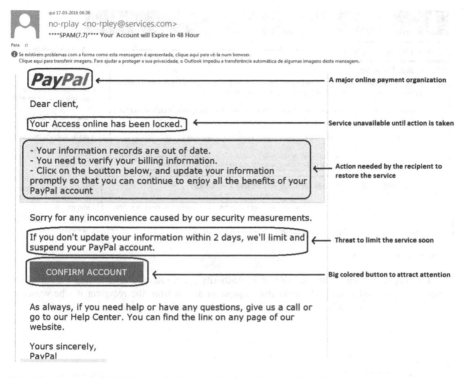

**Fig. 4.1** A scam email using the Authority principle of persuasion. The figure shows an example of a traditional Authority scam category email using the *Authority* principle of persuasion with elements that request urgent action under the pretense to limit the service, if that action is not soon taken

to confirm the sender's legitimacy, including the message's up to date content—paperless statements.

Turning now to other principles of persuasion, among the presented scam categories there are two—*Commitment+Reciprocation+Consistency and Distraction*—that are frequently used together and utilized more frequently than the others. Scammers use these within the email categories of Money Transfer, Business Email Compromise and Sales, among others. The latter two are scam categories on the rise (Fig. 2.5). In situations where money transfer and reciprocation of business commitments are required, these two principles of persuasion work well.

Figure 4.3 presents an email sent by what appears to be a known travel company regarding a flight booking. This email uses the principle of *Commitment+Reciprocation +Consistency* since it asks for a *reciprocation* from the recipient (opening a file with the reservation) according to his/her previous action (*consistency*) which in this case was (not) to book a specific flight. Regardless of the recipient's actions prior to receiving the email, i.e., whether or not a travel reservation has previously been made, the *Distraction* principle guarantees a heightened inclination to perform the required action, either to make sure there is no mistake or to ascertain if some sort of prize or gift is being offered. Alternatively,

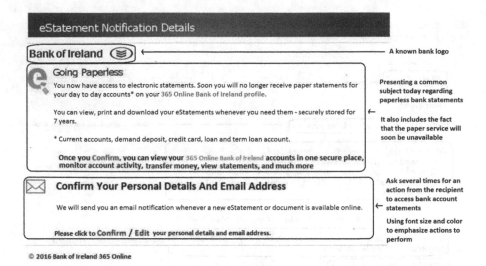

**Fig. 4.2** The figure shows an example of an Authority scam category email using the *Authority* principle of persuasion with elements that request an action from the recipient if s/he wants to access bank statements online, as these will no more be available on paper

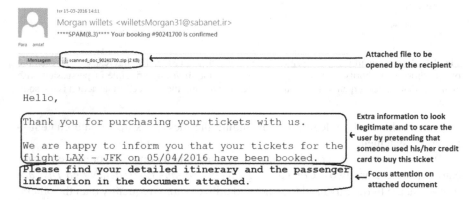

**Fig. 4.3** A scam email using the Commitment+Reciprocity+Consistency and Distraction principles of persuasion. The figure shows an example of a Sales category scam email using the principles of: *Commitment+Reciprocation+Consistency*—asking to open a file and *Distraction*—giving detailed information on the pretense reservation

the email could also generate the fear in the recipient that his/her credit card has been fraudulently used to buy this ticket. The recipient would then be more willing to click on the attachment for clarification. Other elements that express the *Distraction* principle in this email message are: the attached file, the message in bold focusing attention on accessing the file, and the detailed, legitimate sounding flight reservation information. Each of the elements of this compact email uses specific persuasion principles to support the common goal of inducing a specific action

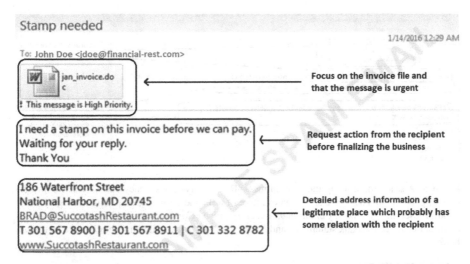

Stamp needed

1/14/2016 12:29 AM

To: John Doe <jdoe@financial-rest.com>

jan_invoice.doc

! This message is High Priority.

Focus on the invoice file and that the message is urgent

I need a stamp on this invoice before we can pay. Waiting for your reply. Thank You

Request action from the recipient before finalizing the business

186 Waterfront Street
National Harbor, MD 20745
BRAD@SuccotashRestaurant.com
T 301 567 8900 | F 301 567 8911 | C 301 332 8782
www.SuccotashRestaurant.com

Detailed address information of a legitimate place which probably has some relation with the recipient

**Fig. 4.4** A scam email using the Commitment+Reciprocity+Consistency and Distraction principles of persuasion. The figure shows an example of a Business Email Compromise category scam email. It uses the principles: *Commitment+Reciprocation+Consistency*—asking with urgency for the recipient to do some action to get paid and *Distraction*—giving detailed legitimate contact information

from the recipient. Its objectivity and clarity make the message sound legitimate while only leaving the recipient room to perform the requested action if s/he desires further information.

Figure 4.4 shows the targeted category of Business Email Compromise. This type of scam email is trending now and is composed of simple parts that express the principles of *Commitment+Reciprocation+Consistency* and *Distraction*. The former principle is expressed by the elements where the sender asks the recipient to perform an action with some urgency in exchange for payment. The latter principle is expressed with the elements that focus the recipient on the file wherein the action needs to be taken, refer to the high priority of the message, and imply with detailed information that the recipient will be paid by a legitimate place.

Another example of Business Email Compromise focuses on normal banking activity (Fig. 4.5). The recipient is informed that monthly invoices from his/her bank are now sent via email and so s/he needs to open the file attached to have access (*Commitment+Reciprocation+Consistency*). Elements of *Distraction* (requesting feedback if the recipient is dissatisfied; detailed and apparently legitimate contact information) are added to focus the recipient on the action of opening the attached document.

The same two principles (i.e., *Commitment+Reciprocation+Consistency and Distraction*) are also used in the Money transfer scam category, as exemplified in Fig. 4.6. Similar to the well known 419 Nigerian scams, this scam email uses the principle *Commitment+Reciprocation+Consistency* by asking the recipient to respond to the message quickly if s/he wants to receive a large amount of money and uses the principle of *Distraction* by giving detailed information on how she/he

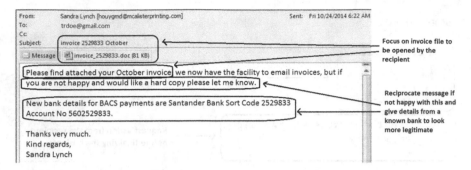

**Fig. 4.5** A scam email using the Commitment+Reciprocity+Consistency and Distraction principles of persuasion. The figure shows an example of a Business Email Compromise category scam email. It uses the principles: *Commitment+Reciprocation+Consistency*—asking the recipient to do some action to see the bank statements and *Distraction*—giving detailed information of a legitimate bank

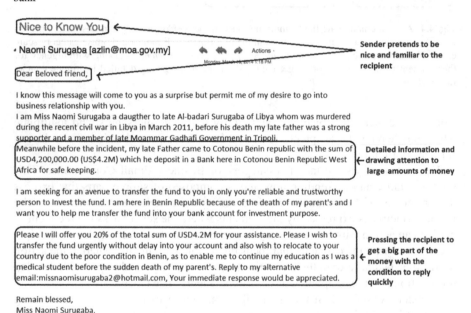

**Fig. 4.6** A scam email using the Commitment+Reciprocity+Consistency and Distraction principles of persuasion. The figure shows an example of a Money Transfer category scam email, also known as a 419 email. It uses the principles: *Commitment+Reciprocation+Consistency*—asking with some urgency to respond to the message if the recipient wants to receive a large amount of money and *Distraction*—giving detailed information on the context in which the recipient was chosen

was chosen and why that substantial amount of money is available to him/her, thus providing perceived legitimacy and context.

While, in general, scam emails use the set of base principles from their associated scam categories, this example shows that specific scam emails can also integrate elements that express other principles to enrich the social presence content and to better achieve the scammers' goals. In this case, the other principle present is the principle of *Liking+Similarity+Deception*, which is expressed with respectful familiarity to the recipient in both the subject and the salutation of the message.

Figure 4.6 has also some similarities with emails from the Romance scam category, which can use, at times, three principles of persuasion: *Commitment+Reciprocation +Consistency*, *Distraction* and *Liking+Similarity+Deception*. In the Romance category, this latter principle is used with the inclusion of personal details that make the email seem more real and thus more reliable. In Romance scams, unlike Money transfer scams, this principle is essential for success, guaranteeing that the social presence goal of this type of scam emails is attained. Scammers try to create an emotional link by pretending to be familiar and to have something in common with the recipient, giving as much detail as possible and in an informal language, so that they can afterwards ask for something in return.

Figure 4.7 shows an example of this type of scam emails. Although they are usually short, they still use the three principles referred above: *Liking+Similarity+Deception*—the sender appears to be familiar and friendly so that it seems there is a real human, with real interests, on the other side; *Commitment+Reciprocation+Consistency*—the sender asks for a reply and an indication of interest; and *Distraction*—the sender provides detailed information about herself, pretending to have real interest in the recipient and to encourage him/her to believe in her trustworthiness.

This type of email has not altered much in the past few years, even though users should be better informed about them and able to easily recognize them. Possibly, scammers have other reasons to still rely upon this type of scam. Perhaps the success rate for these romance scam emails keeps them profitable for scammers. Alternatively, these cruder scam emails may provide a distraction. When recipients

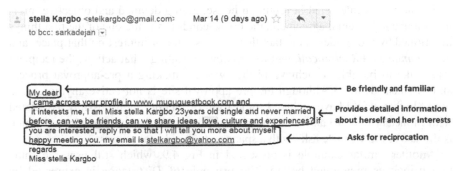

**Fig. 4.7** A scam email using several principles of persuasion. The figure shows an example of a Romance category scam email using the following principles: *Liking+Similarity+Deception*—with a colloquial and familiar tone, *Commitment+Reciprocation+Consistency*—interest in keeping the recipient engaged, and *Distraction*—giving detailed information about personal interests to heighten social context and trustworthiness

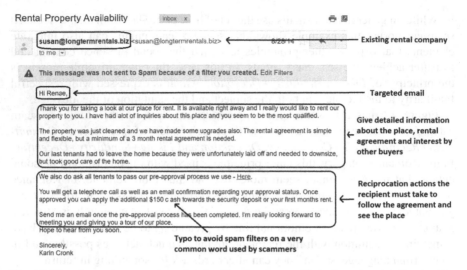

**Fig. 4.8** The figure shows an example of a Rental category (Craigslist) scam email using the following principles: *Commitment+Reciprocation+Consistency* and *Distraction*

compare these romance scams with more crafted, contextualized and seemingly legitimate emails arriving in their mailbox, they may view the latter as more trustworthy than the more obvious scams. Consequently, they may quickly discard the less crafted emails and opt to respond to the more polished ones instead.

Other examples worth mentioning relate to targeted scams which are recent and very common. These are scam emails that take advantage of a well known advertisement company called Craigslist. These emails are connected to Rental and Sales' scam categories and can be easily to target to a specific victim since people need to advertise some contact information whether they are buying or selling.

Figure 4.8 describes a scam type Craigslist email from the Rental scam category. This email uses the principles of *Distraction*: by directing inquest to a specific recipient who is interested in renting a house, giving detailed and objective information about the rental agreement, the house condition while one of the first things mentioned by the sender is the fact that there is a lot of interest on that place; and of *Commitment+Reciprocation+Consistency*: by stating what actions the recipient must take to be able to achieve his/her wishes (making a pre-approval process and payment details.) Although the pre-approval site is not active anymore, it is possible that would have included some form of identity theft possibly associated with monetary loss. To also notice the detail that would probably be ignored which is the use of the word "c ash" with a space so to avoid spam filters.

Another similar example is presented in Fig. 4.9, which still uses the same two principles mentioned before. The principle of *Distraction* is expressed by the use of a targeted address from an apparently known investment company, (notice the almost unnoticeable typo in the sender's email "goldensteinn") and drawing attention to detailed information on home and alternative financing for the rental agreement. The principle of *Commitment+Reciprocation+Consistency* is

**Fig. 4.9** The figure shows an example of a scam email from the Rental category (Craigslist) using the following principles of persuasion: *Commitment+Reciprocation+Consistency* and *Distraction*

**Fig. 4.10** The figure shows an example of a scam email from the Sales category (Craigslist) using the following principles of persuasion: *Commitment+Reciprocation+Consistency* and *Distraction*

again expressed by clearly stating the actions the recipient must take to be able to achieve his/her wishes (either buy or rent the house.)

The example in Fig. 4.10 shows a simple Sales targeted scam email from an ad within the Craigslist site. This type of email is very common, so it is probably re-used many times. To notice that the email refers to an existing/real product in the subject line but the body of its message is very short. This technique allows for the seller to be interested in knowing more about who wants to buy and to do this, s/he needs to use the principle of *Commitment+Reciprocation+Consistency*. Only by reciprocating this email, according to some previous action of posting an item on sale, will the recipient find out more about the sale. Further, the use of a bigger font to make the recipient focusing on the announced product as well as leaving much questions to be answered regarding the interest shown by the sender, make the recipient curious to find out more about how to perform the sale and not properly verify if this can be a scam (using here the *Distraction* principle.)

Another example of Craigslist Sales scam category is described in Fig. 4.11. This example uses mainly the *Distraction* principle to get the interest and attention of the recipient to a well paid job. Although it is mentioned generically the goal of the job, there are not many details onto what really is. The sender mentions good pay, seems to be someone working for the trusted surveys organization (a data entry

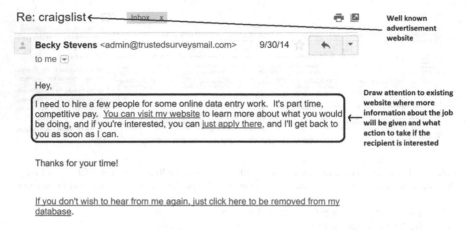

**Fig. 4.11** The figure shows an example of a scam email from the Sales category (Craigslist) using the following principles of persuasion: *Commitment+Reciprocation+Consistency* and *Distraction*

organization) but no more information is available. If the recipient wants to find out more the sender uses the principle of *Commitment+Reciprocation+Consistency* to draw the recipient's attention to an existing website and clearly states what action to take to proceed with the job application.

In all given examples it is clear that, consciously or unconsciously, scammers commonly use specific principles of persuasion in scam emails and adapt them according to the characteristics and goals of each scam category to make those emails more successful. We believe that more effort needs to be put into developing automated techniques to better identify the principles of persuasion found in scam samples. This will help applications enable the user to take the appropriate actions to check the legitimacy of the message and reduce the likelihood of the user to quickly reacting and replying to a scam.

Next we show some examples of how the most used terms and expressions of scam emails have varied over time and how principles of persuasion relate to them.

### 4.2.2  Scam Terms: Trends and Persuasion

After associating principles of persuasion with scam email categories, we want to explore in more detail the content of those emails. To do this, the most used terms in the emails were chosen by tokenizing their content (i.e., dividing a text into its smaller parts until we reach single terms/words.)

Due to the large volume of data, the presented results refer only to the fifty most frequently used terms separately, in pairs (two words used together) or in triples (three words used together.) This grouping allows identification of the use of clusters of terms within the same email and enables analysis of how these can reinforce the expression of specific principles of persuasion. Gathering terms within the sample itself avoids limiting scam email content to a predefined list of words, so the analysis can focus on words that are actually used.

Next we describe the two examples of triples clusters that stood out in the analysis.

In the first example, the triples of terms most frequently used in a single email message are related with large sums of money, money transfer, banks and linked to the United States (Fig. 4.12). The use of these expressions is clearly linked to the Authority scam category (which includes the Bank and the Government subcategories) as well as to the Money Transfer category (which includes, among others, the Charity and the Dead Person and Next of Kin categories.) These scam categories commonly use the principles of *Authority*, *Commitment+Reciprocation+Consistency* and *Distraction*, which provide a high persuasive power. It is also relevant to see which specific terms within the sample heighten scams' effectiveness (e.g., making reference to high amounts of money, banks or to a Country/Government.) Understanding clustering of terms is important in the context of automatically identifying and blocking scam messages, as will be described in Chap. 7.

In the second example, six triples have a very high usage between 2006 and 2008, but then decrease significantly thereafter. While they are used very little in most recent years, they are still present (Fig. 4.13). These terms are mostly

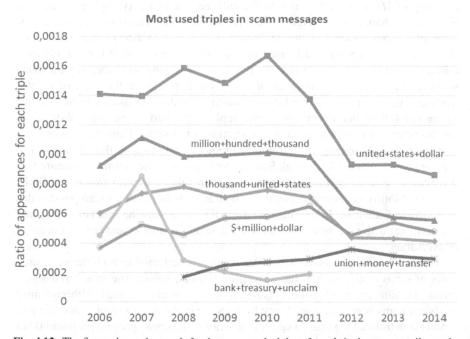

**Fig. 4.12** The figure shows the trends for the most used triples of words in the scam email sample

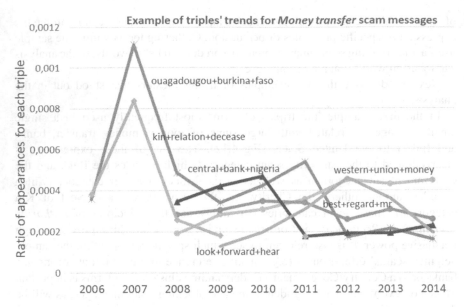

**Fig. 4.13** The figure shows the trends of triples used in 419 scam emails

related with Africa, Burkina Faso or its capital Ouagadougou, African banks and Western Union together with unclaimed funds. They are clearly linked with the scam category of *Money transfer*, mainly the subcategories Charity, Dying Person and Window, Orphan, Refugee. Again, these terms and related categories mainly use the principles of persuasion *Commitment+Reciprocation+Consistency* and *Distraction*. Why were these type of emails used so much in a short period of time, while their current usage is so low? We suggest that better targeting and more sophisticated scam emails increase the number of victims and accelerate the pace of results, making these scams more fruitful than waiting for the few most gullible victims to answer 419 scams. From first victim reply to the end of the scam, 419 scams can involve a lot of effort and time for scammers to pursue. Even when scammers manage to initially engage a victim, they are not certain to keep the victim hooked long enough to achieve their goal. Several iterations with the victim are required, so it makes sense to enter into correspondence with only those who are most gullible. "Since gullibility is unobservable, the best strategy is to get those who possess this quality to self-identify" [8]. So the initial email is effectively the attacker's classifier: it determines who responds, and thus who the scammer attacks and engages in email conversation.

To complement this analysis, similar results are reflected in both the most used pairs of terms over time and the most used separate terms. The most used single terms over time are: bank, fund, account, money, contact and email. Although most analyzed terms have had a tendency to decrease in the most recent years, the pair gmail+com (related to scam category Authority with subcategory Organization) has increased significantly in the last 2 years.

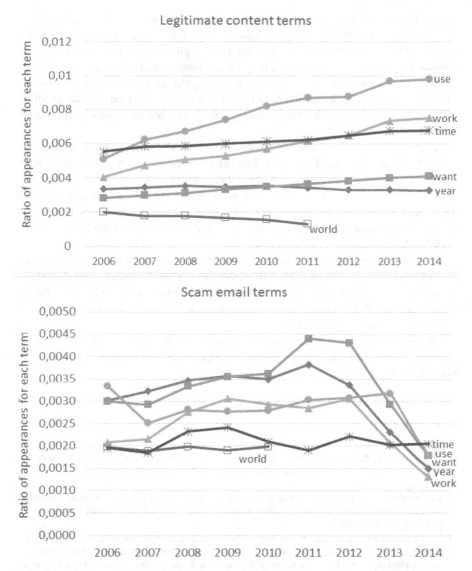

**Fig. 4.14** The figure shows the ratio of each term calculated from the total of the sample between 2006 and 2014. Terms from legitimate content (*top*) (7 most used terms over this period) have almost no variation and denote a recent increase while the same terms in scam emails (*bottom*) are much less used and denote more variations over time, with a recent high decrease in use

### 4.2.3 Comparison Between Scam and Legitimate Term Trends

Once we analyze scam terms it is useful to compare their usage with the same legitimate terms to see if they are used differently over time, i.e., if the same terms are used the same amount of times, if they are constantly used or if they are grouped with similar terms. If their usage trends are different we can use this knowledge to find novel ways to distinguish scam from legitimate messages. For privacy reasons we did not have access to a pool of legitimate emails. Instead, we analyzed the use of similar terms and expressions in legitimate reviews, specifically the Amazon reviews [15], including about 30M Amazon reviews on various products and Amazon services, which integrate legitimate text data set spanning from 2006 to 2014.

A small example shows the behavior over time of the seven most used terms in the legitimate sample (Fig. 4.14). The same terms are much less used in scam emails (ratio values in the $Y$-axis in Fig. 4.14). Further, usage in scam emails varies a lot over the years. The terms were used with greater frequency between 2010 and 2012, but have shown a great decline in the past 2 years. For the legitimate sample, the same terms have been constantly used over the same period of time, with a slight tendency to increase lately (Fig. 4.14).

Thus, the same terms have not the same usage and are not grouped the same way in scam emails and in analyzed legitimate content. Detecting this difference in pattern use for the same terms in scam and legitimate content may be useful for identifying and differentiating, in a more automated fashion, both types of email messages that use the same terms.

The focus of this chapter has been on the *content* of an email, as opposed to whom it appears to be from; that aspect is *another* angle of persuasion, and is described in more detail in Chap. 11.

# References

1. M. Blythe, H. Petrie, J.A. Clark,  F for fake: four studies on how we fall for phish,  in *Proceedings of the SIGCHI Conference on Human Factors in Computing Systems* (ACM, 2011), pp. 3469–3478
2. M. Boodaei,  Mobile users three times more vulnerable to phishing attacks.  Trusteer Technical Report. https://securityintelligence.com/mobile-users-3-times-more-vulnerable-to-phishing-attacks/ (2011)
3. R.B. Cialdini, *Influence: The Psychology of Persuasion* (Harper Business, New York, 2006)
4. A. Ferreira, L. Coventry, G. Lenzini,  Principles of persuasion in social engineering and their use in phishing,  in *Human Aspects of Information Security, Privacy, and Trust* (Springer, Berlin, 2015), pp. 36–47
5. I. Fette, N. Sadeh, A. Tomasic,  Learning to detect phishing emails, in *Proceedings of the 16th International Conference on World Wide Web* (ACM, 2007), pp. 649–656
6. D. Gragg, *A Multi-Level Defense Against Social Engineering* (SANS institute, Swansea, 2003)
7. B. Harrison, A. Vishwanath, Y.J. Ng, R. Rao,  Examining the impact of presence on individual phishing victimization,  in *2015 48th Hawaii International Conference on System Sciences (HICSS)* (IEEE, 2015), pp. 3483–3489
8. C. Herley,  Why do Nigerian Scammers say they are from Nigeria? in *The Workshop on the Economics of Information Security (WEIS)* (2012)
9. J. Hong, The state of phishing attacks. Commun. ACM **55**(1), 74–81 (2012)
10. T.N. Jagatic, N.A. Johnson, M. Jakobsson, F. Menczer,  Social phishing.  Commun. ACM **50**(10), 94–100 (2007)

11. M. Jakobsson, The human factor in phishing, in *Privacy and Security of Consumer Information.* http://markus-jakobsson.com/papers/jakobsson-psci07.pdf (2007)

12. P. Kumaraguru, S. Sheng, A. Acquisti, L.F. Cranor, J. Hong, Teaching Johnny not to fall for phish. ACM Trans. Internet Technol. **10**(2), 7 (2010)

13. S.J. Martin, N. Goldstein, R. Cialdini, *The Small Big: Small Changes that Spark Big Influence* (Profile books Ltd, London, 2014)

14. McAfee Labs threats report, McAfee Inc., Santa Clara, CA. Available: http://www.mcafee.com/us/resources/reports/rp-quarterlythreat-q1-2014.pdf (2014)

15. J. McAuley, J. Leskovec, Hidden factors and hidden topics: understanding rating dimensions with review text, in *Proceedings of the 7th ACM Conference on Recommender Systems* (ACM, 2013), pp. 165–172

16. K.D. Mitnick, W.L. Simon, *The Art of Deception: Controlling the Human Element of Security* (Wiley, New York, 2011)

17. S. Srikwan, M. Jakobsson, Using cartoons to teach internet security. Cryptologia **32**(2), 137–154 (2008)

18. F. Stajano, P. Wilson, Understanding scam victims: seven principles for systems security. Commun. ACM **54**(3), 70–75 (2011)

# Part III
# Filtering Technology

# Chapter 5
# Traditional Countermeasures to Unwanted Email

**Abstract**  This chapter delivers an overview of traditional mechanisms to detect and stop unwanted emails. These mechanisms include email authentication (e.g., DKIM, SPF, DMARC), blacklisting (e.g., DNSBL), and content-based spam filtering (e.g., Naive Bayes Classifier). We explain the extent to which they can be useful to block scam, and point out evasion techniques that help spammers and scammers survive.

## 5.1  The History of Spam

The history of spam is not long, but very eventful. The first commercial email spam message was sent in 1994, by Canter and Siegel, two Arizona lawyers looking for clients interested in obtaining a U.S. Green Card. Directed to several thousand newsgroups, the message immediately angered so many that the ISP of the two attorneys terminated the connection of the offenders within days. Canter and Siegel turned to make money in a different way—by publishing *"How to Make a Fortune on the Information Superhighway: Everyone's Guerrilla Guide to Marketing on the Internet and Other On-Line Services,"* which soon became a source of inspiration to others eyeing the Internet for opportunity. Jeff Slaton, whose nickname later came to be "The Spam King" took this opportunity—first by sending out spam messages of his own, and later by offering his services to others. As Slaton's ISP services were repeatedly terminated, he started to develop methods to circumvent automatic blocking techniques developed by the ISPs. Using throw-away accounts and open-relay email servers, he started the arms race with the service providers.

To counter unwanted emails, the service providers started to scan the content, first looking for digests associated with previous spam messages and later by considering keywords. As service providers started blocking large quantities of messages containing spam keywords, spammers quickly countered by morphing the keywords. A good example of this comes from Pharma spam, whose commercial success in the mid-2000s caused its rapid rise in volume to over three quarters of all spam, when the spammers started using "V ! @ g.r A" and similar mutations instead of "Viagra" to bypass content-based spam filtering. It did not matter to the spammers—whose goal was simply to sell products—that the recipients of their emails understood that the messages were spam.

M. Jakobsson (ed.), *Understanding Social Engineering Based Scams*,
DOI 10.1007/978-1-4939-6457-4_5

To provide more robust anti-spamming mechanisms, service providers started using machine learning for content-based spam filtering. Other approaches including IP blacklisting, email source authentication (e.g., SPF, DKIM, DMARC), behavioral detection (e.g., volume of messages a sender originates), and engagement metrics (what recipients commonly do to the messages—e.g., open the message, place it in the spam folder, add sender to address book, etc) are also utilized for spam detection.

To bypass these detection approaches, spammers introduced polymorphic, image-based, Unicode, and salted spam. To evade IP backlisting and behavioral-based approaches, spammers exploit botnets [35] giving them a large pool of changing IP addresses to send spam, and use the "snowshoe spam" strategy (sending emails in small batches and rotating used IP addresses) to avoid being noticed. Moreover, they use techniques such as *IP hijacking* (also referred to as BGP hijacking) to spoof the source IP of the senders and *chosen message replay* to bypass authentication mechanisms.

Nowadays, unwanted emails include not only advertising spam, but also *Trojan* and *scam* emails (see Fig. 5.1). Trojan emails use spamming mechanisms to distribute harmful attachments or links causing the downloading of malicious executables [19, 39]. Scam emails defraud the recipients using social engineering techniques. In a phishing attack, personal and banking credentials are stolen by a

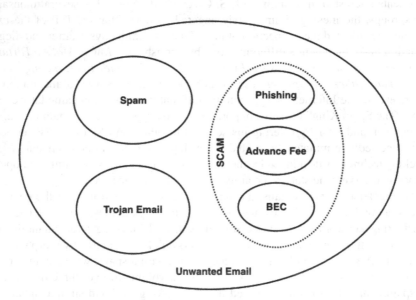

**Fig. 5.1** Classification of unwanted email. Unwanted emails can be categorized into *spam* (selling a product or service), *Trojan email* (distributing malware using an attachment or a malicious link), and *scam* (deceiving users mostly with financial motives). Phishing emails steal credentials (e.g., passwords, credit card); Advance fee (e.g., 419 scam) has different themes including retail-based fraud, stock scams, and work-at-home scams; and Business Email Compromise (BEC) impersonates an employee to commit fraud

website masquerading as a legitimate business (e.g., PayPal, Bank of America). By the beginning of 2004, phishers had become very successful, victimizing online banking sites and their customers. *Advance fee scam*, also known as 419 or Nigerian scam, deceives victims into paying a fee for a service that they will never receive. The most common type of this attack used to ask victims for help in recovering a large sum of money in return for a significant cut. This type of scam being very promising, scammers developed several forms of advance fee scam including inheritance, lottery, dating-romance, death threat, work at home schemes, stock, and retailed-based scams [26, 31]. The overall loss caused by advance fee scam was reported to be $12 billion in 2013 [31].

The most recent and surging type of scam email is *Business Email Compromise* (BEC), which uses compromised business emails to conduct unauthorized fund transfer. BEC has several schemes including "the bogus invoice" in which a customer of a company receives an invoice with an instruction for wire transfer to the fraudster's account, and "CEO Fraud" in which an employee is commanded, using the compromised email, to transfer funds to criminals. The total loss caused by BEC in 2015 is reported $1.2 billion [8].

In this chapter, we sketch the landscape of the most common anti-spamming approaches, and discuss their weaknesses and the evasion techniques employed by attackers. In particular, we consider the efficiency of these measures with respect to scam.

## 5.2  Anti-Spam Landscape

In 2015, Symantec [32] estimated the number of spam emails circulated on the Internet to be approximately 28 billion, equivalent to 60 % of all email traffic. To build a spam distribution network that is resilient against spam detection, spammers rely heavily on networks of compromised machines. It is reported that 74 % of the spam traffic is distributed by botnets. The peer-to-peer botnet Kelihos itself was responsible for 52 % of all spam traffic.

Figure 5.2 depicts a simplified flow of a spam message from source to destination. In this journey, a compromised machine uses a *delivery list, spam template*, and *name dictionary* to generate the spam message and send it to a mail submission agent (MSA). The MSA finds the IP address of the mail transfer agent (MTA) by looking up the Domain Name Server (DNS) of the receiver. Using Simple Mail Transfer Protocol (SMTP), the MSA sends the email to the MTA. The spam may route through several other MTAs to reach the user's inbox.

While routed from the source to the destination, there are a number of places at which spam can be stopped. The first spot is the MSA, which can refuse to relay spam messages. This is done by rate limiting the number of messages accepted from a sender, blacklisting IP addresses of spam bots, or discovering compromised email accounts. The second spot is the MTA, which is able to apply a number of techniques (e.g., blacklisting, SPF, DKIM, and DMARC) to validate senders of emails. In addition, the MTA can limit the volume of spam using gray-listing and challenge

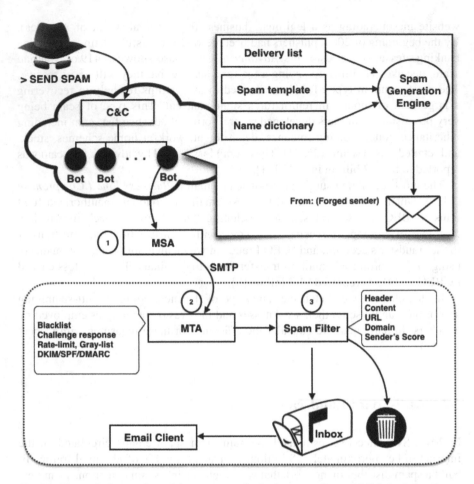

**Fig. 5.2** The typical spam flow. A bot creates and submits an email to a Mail Submission Agent (MSA) using Simple Mail Transfer Protocol (SMTP). The MSA finds the IP address of the domain's Mail Transfer Agent (MTA) by looking up the domain's DNS server and sends the spam. The spam may route through several other MTAs and pass through spam filters. If detected as spam in spots 1–3, it gets discarded or sent to the spam box. The spam often sent out using botnets managed from a command and control (C&C) node

response mechanisms. Finally, spam filters are able to classify spam based on a combination of features including text, link, structure, and social network analysis of email recipients.

These approaches together, can detect large and medium scale spam campaigns where there are strong signals such as repeated contents, URLs, and senders' IP addresses. However, some types of scam messages remain undetected for several reasons. First, these scams target a small population of victims and are sent using IP addresses that are not listed in the blacklist. The IP addresses remain undetected due to the low volume of messages. Second, tweaked contents that are able to bypass the existing content-based spam filtering mechanisms, due to the small volume of such emails, are being used. Finally, some types of scams use stolen credentials or pseudonyms provided by service providers to communicate with users via authenticated channels. Spear-phishing, CEO Fraud, and Craigslist Scam are examples of these types of unwanted emails.

## 5.3 Content-Based Spam Filtering

Spam emails commonly contain signal words such as "For free", "Call now", and "Lowest price" that occur more frequently relative to ham (emails that are neither spam nor scam.) Given a corpus of ham and spam emails, one can compute the probability that a keyword appears in spam. Content-based spam filtering techniques use this statistical feature for *spam classification*.

A common content-base spam classifier that is widely used in commercial and open-source spam-blocking software is the Naive-Bayes algorithm. To compute the odds that an email is spam, it multiplies together the individual odds of each word being spam vs. non-spam, and multiplies that times the overall (prior) odds [25]. More precisely, an email $E$ can be presented as a bag of words [2] $\{w_1, w_2, \ldots, w_n\}$ where each word $w_i$ has the probability $p(w_i|spam)$ of appearing in spam emails and $p(w_i|ham)$ of appearing in ham emails. The following formula shows the simplest version of the Naive Bayes formula to compute the spam score $S$ for the email:

$$S = \frac{p(spam|E)}{p(ham|E)} = \frac{p(w_1|spam) * p(w_2|spam) * \ldots * p(w_n|spam) * p(spam)}{p(w_1|ham) * p(w_2|ham) * \ldots * p(w_n|ham) * p(ham)}$$

In the formula above, $p(ham)$ and $p(spam)$ are the fractions of ham and spam emails, respectively, in a given dataset. If $S$, the odds that email $E$ is spam, is greater than 1, email $E$ most likely is a spam email. Businesses and important communications rely on delivery of emails, so the cost of misclassification of a normal email as spam is high. Therefore, the spam score threshold used is usually greater than 1 to optimize the cost-benefit of spam-filtering.

Other text-classification algorithms that are being used for spam filtering include RIPPER rule induction [10], Support Vector Machines (SVM) [15], Memory-based Learning [29], AdaBoost [9], and Maximum Entropy [37] classifiers. Among these classifiers, SVM, AdaBoost, and Maximum Entropy classifiers have been shown to perform better than others [38].

Text classifiers are content-sensitive and the choice of words has significant impact on their performance. Spammers take advantage of this characteristic to evade classifiers by *polymorphic spam* (same email with a different wording). Polymorphism is different from character substitution, which is described in Chap. 6.

Spammers take different approaches to generate polymorphic spam. The simplest approach is to use polymorphic spam templates. An example of a polymorphic spam

---

[Howdy/Hi there/Hey there/Hi/Hello/Hey]!

Someone in my [Myspace/Facebook] group shared this [site/website] with us so I came to [give it a look/look it over/take a look/check it out]. I'm definitely [enjoying/loving] the information.

I'm [book-marking/bookmarking] and will be tweeting this to my followers!
[Terrific/Wonderful/Great/Fantastic/Outstanding/Exceptional/Superb/Excellent] blog and [wonderful/terrific/brilliant/amazing/great/excellent/fantastic /outstanding/ superb] [style and design/design and style/design].

[I love/I really like/I enjoy/I like/Everyone loves] what you guys [are/are usually/tend to be] up too.
[This sort of/This type of/Such/This kind of] clever work and [exposure/coverage/ reporting]!

Keep up the [superb/terrific/very good/great/good/awesome/fantastic/excellent/ amazing/wonderful] works
guys I've [incorporated/added/included] you guys to [my/our/my personal/my own] blogroll.

---

**Fig. 5.3** A polymorphic spam template. This is a template for a polymorphic spam that generates a spam instance by randomly selecting one word from each placeholder

template is given in Fig. 5.3. Karlberger et al. [22] have studied the effectiveness of a polymorphic spam generator that replaces the spam words with their synonyms. Experimenting on SpamAssassin, DSPAM, and Gmail, they have shown this improves the penetration of spam by 20 %.

*Random word attack* is another polymorphism approach that adds a few random words to reduce the spam score of an email. However, due to the randomness of chosen words which itself can signify a spam message, the success of this approach is limited [17, 24, 36]. *Common word attack* [34] and *Good word attack* [24] offer improvements over this technique by picking words from normal words or those that are frequent in ham emails. It is estimated that by adding 150 common words, spam can evade statistical spam filtering techniques. However, these approaches generate longer email messages, which itself can signify a spam message. Palka and McCoy [27] have proposed and evaluated a new approach for generating scam emails using generative grammars. They demonstrated majority of such emails (85–100 %) bypass current text-base spam filtering systems.

Another approach to disabling text classifiers is to use image instead of text. A variation of this approach uses a mixture of chunks of good texts overlaying a background image with spam words. The spam email then will be readable for end users but not detectable by spam filters [7]. Several approaches strive to defeat this type of spam. For example, Optical Character Recognition (OCR) is used to extract the text from image for text classification. Other approaches including near duplicate detection [33] and content obfuscation detection [6] are also used to detect image-based spam.

Using different unicode characters, attackers create identical looking messages to bypass word matching algorithms [23] (see Chap. 6 ). *Salting* is yet another evasion technique that deludes spam filtering algorithms by adding or distorting content of delivered emails while preserving their appearance [4]. For instance, *hidden salting* conceals random strings by changing their color or placing them after the end of $< /html >$ tag [5].

To overcome the evasion techniques, content-based spam filters usually integrate other features such as email header (e.g., IP address of sender), links (e.g., pattern and reputation of URLs), and email structure to improve their scoring system and accuracy. However, for detecting scams, these additional features are not highly beneficial due to the low volume of scams and absence of strong signals, as described earlier.

## 5.4 Blacklisting Approaches

A large proportion of spam email is sent by spambots through open-relays (MSAs that send emails without authentication) or standalone email agents. A list of IP addresses known to send spam constitutes a blacklist. Several components of email infrastructure including MSA, MTA, or content-based spam filtering software consult with the blacklists to score emails. For example, SpamAssassin uses thirty-five blacklists and employs the results in the scoring of emails [20]. Large ISPs use the most reputable blacklists such as SpamCop, Spamhaus and URIBL.

Blacklists are formed by various entities using different approaches including active probing, manual entry (spam reported by users), passive monitoring, and honey accounts [21]. Another valuable source for listing spamming IP addresses is content-based spam filters. Active probing approaches scan Internet IP addresses to find MSAs that relay emails without authenticating the senders (i.e., open relays). Passive monitoring is based on fake but monitored email agents (MSAs and MTAs) planted only to trap connecting spambots. Fake email addresses known as honey accounts attract spam and add the IP addresses of senders to the blacklist .

A blacklist can be downloaded (e.g., OpenBSD's spamd) or queried as a service. The latter extensively uses DNS infrastructure to disseminate the blacklist records. This type of blacklist is called DNSBL where the inverse of each IP address (or subnet) appears in the form of an A record ([Inverse IP].blacklist_name). The inverse of the IP address is used in the A record, instead of the IP, to allow hierarchical and network level blacklisting. Email agents check the existence of an IP in the blacklist using DNS lookup [20]. First, the inverse of the sender's IP address is computed (e.g., 23.42.168.192 is obtained from 192.168.42.23.) Then, [inverse ip].blacklist_name (23.42.168.192.blacklist_name.) is queried from DNS server. This will return either an address, indicating that the sender's IP is in the balcklist; or "NXDOMAIN" code (i.e., No such domain) implying that IP is not blacklisted [11, 12].

Blacklisting has profound effect on controlling bulk unwanted emails. Jung and Sit [20] and Katich et al. [21] independently reported that IP addresses of 80 % of spam sent to a university network in 2004 and a botnet in 2008 respectively have appeared in at least one blacklist. The latter work measured the median time for a spambot to appear in a blacklist to be 1.5 h.

To counter the blacklist, botnets frequently delist bots after they appear in the blacklists [21] or quickly rotate domains and recirculate IP addresses to avoid blacklisting techniques from identifying their traffic. They also spread the workload of sending very short bursts of spam over several bots [18]. This is commonly known as the "Snowshoe spam" strategy. Moreover, spammers can hijack IP addresses of reputable networks and use them to send spam without being caught by blacklisting techniques. Spammers achieve IP hijacking by announcing unauthorized network prefixes when an ISP does not filter *Border Gateway Protocol* (BGP) routing advertisements or using a man-in-the-middle attack on an ISP-to-ISP BGP session. Using this technique, they gain possession of IP addresses of a valid autonomous system (a collection of connected IPs under the control of a network operator) that are not blacklisted. Ramachandran and Feamster [28] measured the volume of spam sourced from hijacked IPs to be around 10 %.

## 5.5   Anti-Spoofing Approaches

Spoofing is not about *delivering* messages, but rather, about having them *appear credible*. This is less relevant in the context of spam, of course, than in the context of scam.

Simple Mail Transfer Protocol (SMTP) does not authenticate the sender of emails. Therefore, a spammer can send an email pretending to be from a made-up or existing email address. This is called spoofing and is mostly used by spammers to masquerade as a reputable entity. To overcome this problem, anti-spamming approaches are proposed to authenticate the senders. In this section we describe some of these approaches as well as spammers' evasion techniques.

### 5.5.1   DKIM

DomainKey Identified Mail (DKIM) is a cryptographic method for email integrity check and authentication using public key infrastructure and digital signature [14]. Using this method, email messages are signed by the private key of the sending domain. The receiver domain verifies the signature of the email using the public key of the sender domain available through DNS. Contrary to end-to-end protocols, DKIM only verifies emails at the border of domains without end clients being involved. It is reported that 83 % of traffic received by Gmail contained a DKIM signature, but 6 % failed to be validated due to weak cryptographic keys, revoked

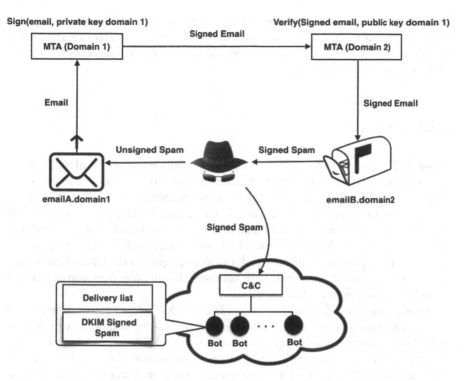

**Fig. 5.4** Steps in an attack against DKIM. In a chosen message replay attack against DKIM, the spammer creates two email accounts in domain 1 and domain 2 (e.g., Gmail and Yahoo domains). Then, he composes a spam message (unsigned spam) using the email account of domain 1 to be sent to his account in domain 2. The MTA of the sender domain signs the content of the email along with the sender's email address using the private key of the sender domain. The destination domain receives and verifies the signature of the email using the public key of the sender domain. Finally the signed version of the message will be delivered to the spammer's account in the domain 2. Since the receiver's email address is not included in the signature, the spammer can replace the receiver's address and send it to several recipients

keys, protocol errors, or signature failure (18 % of the cases). The remaining 17 % of the traffic, mostly coming from unknown service providers, do not use DKIM and remain open to spoofing.

Sender domains that use DKIM are not completely spoof-proof due to vulnerabilities such as "Chosen Message Replay". In this attack, the spammer obtains a signed version of the spam email by sending the email to himself or an accomplice. Since DKIM does not include email address of the receiver in the signature, the spammer can replace the email address of receiver and send spam to thousands of users [1]. Figure 5.4 shows the steps of this attack.

DKIM is used by machines to authenticate the sender of email messages. Scammers use social engineering techniques such as *display name abuse* and *look-alike domain name attack* to evade DKIM[1]. In the display name abuse, spammers use an arbitrary email address with a display name pretending to be authentic (e.g., From: "Important Manager" <whiplash@example.org>). In the look-alike domain name attack, attackers use domain names similar to masqueraded service (e.g., a message from <customer@PayPa1.com> where the last character of the domain is the digit one).

## 5.5.2  SPF

Using SMTP, attackers can easily spoof a sender address of an email and make it appear to be sent from a legitimate domain. To limit this capability, Sender Policy Framework (SPF) [30] has provided a simple mechanism to validate the origin IP addresses of emails. In this approach, the sender domain provides the list of authorized IP addresses (or CIDR block of IPs) from the domain that are allowed to send out emails. This list is distributed by DNS infrastructure through DNS records of the sender. Upon receiving an email, the receiver queries the DNS of the sender domain to find the list of authorized IP addresses. Emails sent from non-authorized IP addresses are considered as spam.

As an example, the DNS record "example.com. TXT 'v=spf1 a:mail.example.com -all'" means that example.com domain only authorizes the computer with domain name "mail.example.com" to send its emails. When a MTA receives an email from "example.com", it looks up the SPF records of the sender's DNS and accepts the email only if the IP address of the sender matches the "mail.example.com". If there is no SPF record in the DNS of sender, it potentially means that the sender domain does not support SPF.

Studies show that 92 % of Gmail's inbound traffic use SPF. However, only 47 % of top million Alexa domains publish SPF policies. Of those, 34 % provide IP ranges, 64 % use A or MX mechanisms (if the sender domain name has an A/MX record matching the sender name). About 2 % of domains delegate the SPF policies of their domains to other service providers. These domains include redirection to few well-known cloud email providers such as Yandex (36 %) and mailhostbox.com (17 %) [16]. Migration to cloud services with shared infrastructure is a major concern for the current design of SPF since a malicious host can spoof emails of other tenants. Moreover, spammers can spoof emails from a domain with an SPF policy using a compromised machine in the domain, a hijacked email account, or BGP hijacking. Using BGP hijacking, spammers take over the range of IP addresses they want to spoof to send fake but SPF validated emails [3].

In comparison with DKIM, which provides authentication and integrity, SPF only provides a method for authentication of email senders. While DKIM enables authentication by signing content of emails, SPF does so by verifying the senders' IP addresses. These two methods are complementary and cover a wider range of attack scenarios such as spamming by BGP hijacking and chosen message replay. However, none of these methods offer protection against spam from hijacked emails, compromised machines, or scam emails that use display name abuse or look-alike domain name attack. This highlights the importance of content-based spam filtering.

### 5.5.3 DMARC

Domain-based Message Authentication, Reporting, and Conformance (DMARC) [13] glues together a number of existing mechanisms including DKIM and SPF. It allows the sender of emails to publish the supported type of email authentication (DKIM/SPF), and to suggest policies and preferences for message validation, disposition, and reporting of failed authentications. Moreover, it provides a mechanism for reporting actions performed under these policies. Senders publish DMARC policies through DNS TXT records (under _dmarc.domain.com) [13].

In 2015, only 26 % of Gmail's inbound traffic came from domains with a published DMARC policy [16]. Even more striking, only 1.1 % of the top million Alexa websites publish DMARC policies. While 81 % of domains support both DKIM and SPF, 11 % support only SPF, and about 2 % support DKIM only. This inconsistency limits the effectiveness of DKIM and SPF.

## References

1. Analysis of Threats Motivating DomainKeys Identified Mail (DKIM) (RFC 4686), https://tools.ietf.org/html/rfc4686#section-4.1.4 (2014). Accessed 17 Apr 2016
2. Bag-of-Words Model, https://en.wikipedia.org/wiki/Bag-of-words_model. Accessed 17 Apr 2016
3. H. Ballani, P. Francis, X. Zhang, A study of prefix hijacking and interception in the internet. ACM SIGCOMM Comput. Commun. Rev. **37**, 265–276 (2007)
4. A. Bergholz, G. Paass, F. Reichartz, S. Strobel, M.-F. Moens, B. Witten, Detecting known and new salting tricks in unwanted emails, in *CEAS* (2008)
5. A. Bergholz, J. De Beer, S. Glahn, M.-F. Moens, G. Paaß, S. Strobel, New filtering approaches for phishing email. J. Comput. Secur. **18**(1), 7–35 (2010)
6. B. Biggio, G. Fumera, I. Pillai, F. Roli, Image spam filtering by content obscuring detection, in *CEAS* (2007)
7. B. Biggio, G. Fumera, I. Pillai, F. Roli, A survey and experimental evaluation of image spam filtering techniques. Pattern Recogn. Lett. **32**(10), 1436–1446 (2011)
8. Business email compromise, http://www.ic3.gov/media/2015/150827-1.aspx (2015). Accessed 17 Apr 2016
9. X. Carreras, L. Màrquez and J.G. Salgado, Boosting trees for anti-apam email filtering, in *Proceedings of RANLP-01, 4th International Conference on Recent Advances in Natural Language Processing*, Tzigov Chark, BG, (2001).
10. W.W. Cohen., Learning rules that classify e-mail, in *AAAI Spring Symposium on Machine Learning in Information Access*, vol. 18 (1996), p. 25
11. DNS blacklists and whitelists, https://tools.ietf.org/html/rfc5782 (2010). Accessed 17 Apr 2016
12. DNSBL, https://en.wikipedia.org/wiki/DNSBL (2010). Accessed 17 Apr 2016
13. Domain-based message authentication, reporting, and conformance (DMARC), https://tools.ietf.org/html/rfc7489 (2015) Accessed 17 Apr 2016
14. DomainKeys Identified Mail (DKIM) Signatures, https://tools.ietf.org/html/rfc6376 (2011) Accessed 17 Apr 2016
15. H. Drucker, D. Wu, V.N. Vapnik, Support vector machines for spam categorization. IEEE Trans. Neural Netw. **10**(5), 1048–1054 (1999)
16. Z. Durumeric, D. Adrian, A. Mirian, J. Kasten, E. Bursztein, N. Lidzborski, K. Thomas, V. Eranti, M. Bailey, J.A. Halderman, Neither snow nor rain nor mitm...: An empirical analysis of

email delivery security, in *Proceedings of the 2015 ACM Conference on Internet Measurement Conference* (ACM, 2015), pp. 27–39

17. J. Graham-Cumming, How to beat an adaptive spam filter, in *Presentation at the MIT Spam Conference* (2004)

18. Internet Security Threat Report (ISTR), https://www.symantec.com/content/dam/symantec/docs/reports/istr-21-2016-en.pdf (2016). Accessed 17 Apr 2016

19. M. Jakobsson, Z. Ramzan, *Crimeware: Understanding New Attacks and Defenses*, 1st edn. (Addison-Wesley Professional, 2008)

20. J. Jung, E. Sit, An empirical study of spam traffic and the use of DNS black lists, in *Proceedings of the 4th ACM SIGCOMM Conference on Internet Measurement* (ACM, 2004), pp. 370–375

21. C. Kanich, C. Kreibich, K. Levchenko, B. Enright, G.M. Voelker, V. Paxson, S. Savage, Spamalytics: an empirical analysis of spam marketing conversion, in *Proceedings of the 15th ACM Conference on CCS* (ACM, 2008)

22. C. Karlberger, G. Bayler, C. Kruegel, E. Kirda, Exploiting redundancy in natural language to penetrate Bayesian spam filters, in *Workshop on Offensive Technologies (WOOT)*, vol. 7 (2007), pp. 1–7

23. C. Liu, S. Stamm, Fighting unicode-obfuscated spam, in *Proceedings of the Anti-phishing Working Groups 2nd Annual eCrime Researchers Summit* (ACM, 2007), pp. 45–59

24. D. Lowd, C. Meek, Good word attacks on statistical spam filters, in *CEAS* (2005)

25. V. Metsis, I. Androutsopoulos, G. Paliouras, Spam filtering with naive Nayes – which naive Bayes? in *CEAS* (2006), pp. 27–28

26. G.R. Newman, R.V. Clarke, *Superhighway Robbery*, Preventing E-commerce Crime, Willan Publishing, Routledge, USA (2013)

27. S. Palka and Damon McCoy. Fuzzing e-mail filters with generative grammars and n-gram analysis, in *9th USENIX Workshop on Offensive Technologies (WOOT)* (2015)

28. A. Ramachandran, N. Feamster, Understanding the network-level behavior of spammers. ACM SIGCOMM Comput. Commun. Rev. **36**(4), 291–302 (2006)

29. G. Sakkis, I. Androutsopoulos, G. Paliouras, V. Karkaletsis, C.D. Spyropoulos, P. Stamatopoulos, A memory-based approach to anti-spam filtering for mailing lists. Inf. Retr. **6**(1), 49–73 (2003)

30. Sender Policy Framework (SPF) for authorizing use of domains in email, version 1, https://tools.ietf.org/html/rfc7208 (2014) Accessed 17 Apr 2016

31. Smart people easier to scam. 419 advance fee fraud statistics 2013, http://www.ultrascan-agi.com/public_html/html/pdf_files/Pre-Release-419_Advance_Fee_Fraud_Statistics_2013-July-10-2014-NOT-FINAL-1.pdf (2013). Accessed 17 Apr 2016

32. Symantec, Internet Security Threat Report (ISRT). https://www4.symantec.com/mktginfo/whitepaper/ISTR/21347931_GA-internet-security-threat-report-volume-20-2015-appendices.pdf (2014). Accessed 17 Apr 2016

33. Z. Wang, W.K. Josephson, Q. Lv, M. Charikar, K. Li, Filtering image spam with near-duplicate detection, in *CEAS* (2007)

34. G.L. Wittel, S.F. Wu, On attacking statistical spam filters, in *CEAS* (2004)

35. Y. Xie, F. Yu, K. Achan, R. Panigrahy, G. Hulten, I. Osipkov, Spamming botnets: signatures and characteristics. ACM SIGCOMM Comput. Commun. Rev. **38**, 171–182 (2008)

36. J. Zdziarski, Bayesian noise reduction: Contextual symmetry logic utilizing pattern consistency analysis, in *Proceedings of the MIT Spam Conference, Cambridge, MA, USA* (2005)

37. L. Zhang, T.-S. Yao, Filtering junk mail with a maximum entropy model, in *Proceeding of 20th International Conference on Computer Processing of Oriental Languages (ICCPOL03)* (2003, pp. 446–453

38. L. Zhang, J. Zhu, T. Yao, An evaluation of statistical spam filtering techniques. ACM Trans. Asian Lang. Inf. Process. **3**(4), 243–269 (2004)

39. C.C. Zou, D. Towsley, W. Gong, Email worm modeling and defense, in *Proceedings of the 13th International Conference on Computer Communications and Networks (ICCCN)* (IEEE, 2004), pp. 409–414

# Chapter 6
# Obfuscation in Spam and Scam

**Abstract** In this chapter, we demonstrate a vulnerability in existing content-based message filtering methods, showing how an attacker can use a simple obfuscator to modify any message to a homograph version of the same message, thereby avoiding digest and signature based detection methods. We measure the success of this potential attack, showing a total success against Hotmail, Gmail and Yahoo mail. While the attack is bothersome both in terms of its simplicity and its success, it is also easily countered. We describe some computationally practical countermeasures.

## 6.1 Confusable Characters and Homograph Scam Attacks

Chapter 5 explained traditional filtering techniques, including reputation-based and content-based filtering. Today, scammers commonly send low-volume quantities of emails from accounts with good (or at least not bad) reputations. They are only starting to try out various approaches to beat content-based filters. This chapter takes a look at what we may expect next on this front.

We believe that the next natural move by the scammers may very well be to use homograph attacks, in which unwanted messages are represented using a collection of encodings that are visually identical in the eyes of the recipients. For example, the small Cyrillic letter *"er"* looks the same as the letter "p" and a word in which the latter is replaced by the former will be visually unaffected, but evade signature-based detection. For each Latin letter, many "confusable" characters exist; the exact number depends on the fonts used and the exactness of visual match desired by the sender. We will demonstrate below the success of this obfuscation technique by showing that common email scam messages that were all blocked in their "raw form" were almost without exception delivered after being obfuscated—whether to Google accounts, Yahoo accounts or Hotmail accounts. This obfuscation, which is not detectable to the human eye, is straightforward to automate; we wrote a simple obfuscator that performs replacements in an input message, creating one or more identical-looking obfuscated output messages—each of which is unique.

© Springer Science+Business Media New York 2016
M. Jakobsson (ed.), *Understanding Social Engineering Based Scams*,
DOI 10.1007/978-1-4939-6457-4_6

| A | 𝔄 | 𝔸 | 𝖀 | 𝒜 | A | 𝒜 |
|---|---|---|---|---|---|---|
| A | *A* | *A* | *A* | A | *A* | A |
| A | A | A | A | A | A | A |
| A | *A* | A | A | A | *A* | |

**Fig. 6.1** Confusable characters for the Latin upper-case "A"

| AFFIRM | AFFIRM | AFF I RM |
|--------|--------|----------|

**Fig. 6.2** Confusable characters for the Latin upper-case "I" inside a word context. The right-most confusable character is (by itself) almost identical to the one on the *left*, but put in context with other characters, it clearly stands out

The use of a randomized compilation of a scam message, performed on a per-transmission basis, allows an attacker to send very large volumes of *visually identical* messages, all while circumventing digest-based volume detection used in spam filters. This would correspond to a polymorphic spam/scam message. This is worth considering, if only because of the success of polymorphic attacks in the context of malware [2].

The Unicode Consortium made available a list of visually similar *confusable* characters [6]—see Fig. 6.1 for an example. However, as the figure shows, characters that are similar may still be easily distinguishable, due to differences in stroke size and the height and length of the characters. Figure 6.2 shows confusable characters for the Latin upper-case "I" embedded in words.

However, while many of the confusable characters can easily be visually distinguished from each other, a fair number of them truly look identical—see Fig. 6.3. Using confusable characters, a scammer can build a simple message obfuscator that takes in as input a block of text and outputs an obfuscated version where the characters are replaced with their corresponding high-fidelity confusable character. If no confusable is available for a character, the original character is preserved. The resulting message appears identical to the original to the human eye, but is in fact encoded very differently.

Based on the distribution of characters in English language, one can compute the per-character entropy increase resulting from performing a compilation in which one of a character's look-alikes (including the correct character) is selected, uniformly at random, for each letter in a word. For example, Fig. 6.3 shows that "E" has two confusables and "z" has one; therefore, each time an "E" is detected, there are three candidate encodings while every time a "z" is detected, there are two. In the former case, the entropy increase would be $log_2(3) \approx 1.58$, whereas in the latter case, the entropy increase is exactly 1. Weighting these by the relative frequency of the character (while, for simplicity) assuming that all characters are used in their lower-case forms only, we get an average entropy increase of approximately 0.73 bits per character, or more than 2000 bits for a typical scam email (whose

| A | B | C | E | F | G | H | K | L | M | N | O | P | R | S | T | U | V | X | Z |
|---|---|---|---|---|---|---|---|---|---|---|---|---|---|---|---|---|---|---|---|
| A | B | C | E | F | G | H | K | L | M | N | O | P | R | S | T | U | V | X | Z |
|   | B |   | E |   |   | H |   | L | M |   | O | P |   |   | T |   |   | X |   |
|   | B |   |   |   |   |   |   |   |   |   |   |   |   |   | T |   |   | X |   |
|   |   | a | c | e |   | i |   | j |   | o | p |   | s | v | w |   | x | z |   |
|   |   | a | c | e |   | i |   | j |   | o | p |   | s | v | w |   | x | z |   |
|   |   |   | c |   |   |   |   | j |   |   |   |   |   | v |   |   |   |   |   |
|   |   |   | c |   |   |   |   |   |   |   |   |   |   |   |   |   |   |   |   |

**Fig. 6.3** Visually indistinguishable confusable characters. The figure shows 48 high-fidelity confusable characters that are visually more or less indistinguishable to their Latin counterpart (shown on the *top row* of each column). That means that if they are used instead of their corresponding Latin letters in an email, this substitution is typically not visually detectable by the recipient. At the same time, traditional content-based filters are thwarted

length, on average, is close to 3,000 characters.) This shows that while it may be possible to enumerate all homograph versions of unique keywords, it is not practically meaningful to do this for snippets of text, and certainly not for entire emails.

## 6.2 How to Test the Attack

Commercial spam filters use a variety of ways to identify unwanted messages, based on factors such as the message body, the sender reputation, URLs in the message, attachments, etc. For example, Gmail's spam filter uses a combination of methods including linear classifiers and artificial neural networks, and claims to block 99.9 % of all spam emails [5]. Below we describe a recent experiment we performed in which the efficacy of three commercial email filters—namely, Gmail, Hotmail and Yahoo mail—was measured when exposed to scam messages obfuscated with confusable characters.

The first step was to select scam messages that are detected and blocked by these three major email providers. We sent over 400 scam messages—traditional 419 scam messages that were common enough for the service providers to write content-based filters for them—from newly registered accounts at each of the three popular email providers, addressed to equally fresh recipient accounts. Ninety messages ended up in the recipients' spam folder [3]. Since both the sender and recipient accounts were new and had no existing reputation, it is likely that the decision made by the email filter was based largely on the message content.

**Table 6.1** Block rate of obfuscated scam messages

|                     | Gmail (recipient) | Hotmail (recipient) | Yahoo (recipient) |
|---------------------|-------------------|---------------------|-------------------|
| Gmail (sender 1)    | 1/90              | 0/89                | 0/90              |
| Gmail (sender 2)    | 1/90              | 1/89                | 2/90              |
| Hotmail (sender 3)  | 1/90              | 0/89                | 0/90              |
| Hotmail (sender 4)  | 0/90              | 0/89                | 0/90              |
| Yahoo (sender 5)    | 20/90             | 0/89                | 0/90              |
| Yahoo (sender 6)    | 19/90             | 0/89                | 0/90              |

The fraction of obfuscated scam messages sent to each recipient that did not reach the recipients inbox from each sender account. A mistake caused only 89 messages (instead of 90) to be sent to the Hotmail account. It is unknown why Gmail manages to catch more obfuscated messages sent from Yahoo than other email providers. Note that, in their non-obfuscated form, these messages *all* were blocked by all three email providers

In a second step, these 90 scam messages were "compiled" using an obfuscator that replaced characters with confusable counterparts. After that, the obfuscated messages were sent from six email accounts (two from each email provider) to three recipients (one from each email provider), all newly registered for the purpose of this experiment. The transmission was paced so as to simulate the low-and-slow behavior of scammers and to avoid triggering rate-limits enforced by the email providers.

Table 6.1 lists the fraction of messages sent to each recipient that did not reach the recipients' inbox from each sender account. 96 % of the sent obfuscated scam messages were successfully delivered. However, the same message from the same sender may not reach all recipients, e.g., Yahoo sender accounts have a much lower success rate to the Gmail recipient than to Hotmail or Yahoo recipients. This shows that the obfuscated scam messages were filtered at inbound time on the recipient side, rather than at outbound time on the sender side. Overall, the block rate of obfuscated scam messages is 7.8 % for the Gmail recipient, 0.4 % for the Hotmail recipient, and 0.2 % for the Yahoo recipient. The low block rate at these three popular email providers suggests that there is little protection against scam messages obfuscated with confusable characters.

## 6.3  Detecting Obfuscated Scam

In 2007, Liu and Stamm [4] studied the use of obfuscated spam messages— without an emphasis on making the obfuscation unnoticeable to the recipient. They suggested using reverse mappings to identify the use of homograph attacks in spam. Here, a reverse mapping is one that maps all characters looking like an "A" to "A", all characters looking like a "B" to a "B", and so on.[1] This is a helpful approach, and can be augmented in several ways to improve the detection:

- It should be recognized that whereas English-language spam and scam messages dominate the Internet email traffic, there is a market for other languages (and character sets) as well—and commonly, filters blocking spam and scam emails for other character sets are not getting the same attention as filters blocking Latin-character abuse does. It is straightforward to scan messages to identify the use of multiple character sets, and to create one output stream for each potential character set that the message could be mapped to. For example, if the first few characters of a message are Latin, and then there are Cyrillic characters, then two obvious candidate mappings would be from Cyrillic to Latin and from Latin to Cyrillic. For most legitimate messages, there would only be one character set, and therefore, no candidate mappings at all. For the small portion of legitimate messages containing multiple character sets, there would be a very low likelihood that the parsed characters would happen to be confusables, and so, the creation of the mappings could be terminated early. For example, if an email contains Latin characters with some words in Chinese, the inclusion of the Chinese characters would not increase the risk score, as none of them look like Latin characters. Once a collection of mapped results have been produced, these can be individually scanned for undesirable content.
- One method to detect polymorphic message streams without requiring the storage of all previously processed messages is to perform the reverse-mapping described above as a normalization step, then to compute a digest for a suitable selection, and maintaining a count for each such selection.
- Whereas content-based scanning is beneficial for detecting many types of spam and scam—especially targeted attacks, where there are few other viable options—it is important to recognize that any content-based method is vulnerable to changes in the message contents. This has been partially addressed by the introduction of story line detection [1]. However, we suggest another, more general approach: by identifying and counting the transitions from one character set to another, it is possible to quantify the likely degree of obfuscation in a message. Therefore, even if the mapped content does not trigger a content-based filter, a risk score can be determined based on the number of transitions. Here, different weights can be given to transitions between sentences and words (both having low weight) than to transitions inside words (high weight), reflecting the likely nature of the homograph abuse. To be precise, only transitions involving characters that are designated as confusables would contribute to the score.

---

[1] This, of course, should only be done to emails that "appear as Latin-character emails"—for emails appearing to be written in Cyrillic, but containing some Latin characters, the mapping would have to be made from Latin to Cyrillic.

# References

1. M. Jakobsson, W. Leddy, AI vs. the Phishers, in *IEEE Spectrum Magazine* (2016)
2. M. Jakobsson, G. Stewart, Mobile malware: why the traditional AV paradigm is doomed, and how to use physics to detect undesirable routines, in *BlackHat* (2013)
3. M. Jakobsson, T.-F. Yen, How vulnerable are we to scams? in *BlackHat* (2015)
4. C. Liu, S. Stamm, Fighting Unicode-Obfuscated Spam, in *APWG eCrime Researchers Summit* (2007)
5. S.H. Somanchi, The mail you want, not the spam you don't. https://gmail.googleblog.com/2015/07/the-mail-you-want-not-spam-you-dont.html (2015)
6. Unicode Technical Standard 39: Unicode Security Mechanisms, http://www.unicode.org/reports/tr39/ (2016)

# Chapter 7
# Semantic Analysis of Messages

**Abstract** This chapter describes a novel content-based detection method based on the semantics—or meaning—of messages. This is a powerful tool since scammers commonly change formulations but rarely change storylines. We use examples related to the stranded traveler scam, which is a common result of account take-overs, whether of email or of Facebook accounts. We note that the same methods can be applied to an array of other types of scams—in fact, all but scams employing extremely short messages and those that do not rely on a fixed storyline, such as some classes of romance scams (see Chap. 10.)

## 7.1 Example: Stranded Traveler Scams

Traditional content-based spam filtering commonly involves the detection of short strings, such as "Viagra", "V ! @ G R A", and short strings of words that are common in spam messages but not in ham,[1] such as the sequence "Urgent Transfer Request for". Another common method identifies messages by their digests, which effectively corresponds to comparing long message portions—or the entire email content—to previously recorded blacklisted segments. Email service providers use this to identify large numbers of messages with identical content. These methods are both poorly suited to address many scam messages. To see why, let's look at two closely related examples of the "stranded traveler" genre. These scams are usually sent from the accounts of somebody the recipient knows, but sent by a scammer who has phished the owner of that account.

---

[1] We use the term "ham" to mean "not spam and not scam", as described in Chap. 5. The common use of the term is simply "not spam".

© Springer Science+Business Media New York 2016
M. Jakobsson (ed.), *Understanding Social Engineering Based Scams*,
DOI 10.1007/978-1-4939-6457-4_7

## 7.2 Detecting Storylines

Consider the emails in Figs. 7.1 and 7.2 from the perspective of traditional filtering methods. To begin with, they come from a trusted party. If the scammer is careful, he avoids transmitting it from an IP address or mail server with a poor reputation. Turning to the content, we can see that the emails naturally avoid common keywords associated with spam. For example, there are no product names associated with mass emails—no mention of "Sex", "Free" or "Rolex", for example. Although the supposed geographic location of the sender usually comes from a relatively limited number of places, of which London and Manila often figure, geographic locations do not typically indicate unwanted email. Furthermore, an email digest based scan

---

**Subject: Emergency!**
Hello,
How are you doing? I hope this message finds you please get
back to me as soon as you received this (It's a matter of
Urgency). I'm in a terrible situation. I came down here to
Manila, Philippines for a program, last night on my way back
to my hotel room I was robbed at gunpoint, my wallet and other
valuables were stolen off me, leaving my passport and life
safe. I will appreciate whatever you can assist me with. Let
me know if you can be of help.

Thanks,
Robert Lee

---

**Fig. 7.1** Example 1, stranded traveler scam. This is a first example of a strander traveler scam email

---

**Subject: Sad News...........................John Owens**
I'm writing this with tears in my eyes,My family and i came
down here to London,England for a short vacation and we were
mugged at gun point last night at the park of the hotel where
we lodged all cash,credit cards and cell phone were stolen
off us.I've been to the US embassy and the Police here but
they're not helping issues at all,My flight leaves in hew hrs
from now and am having problems settling the hotel bills.The
hotel manager won't let me leave until i settle the hotel bills
now...Well I really need your financial assistance..Please,
Let me know if you can help us out? Am freaked out at the
Moment.John Owens.......

---

**Fig. 7.2** Example 2, stranded traveler scam. This is a second example of a strander traveler scam email. Whereas the two scams are likely to originate from two different scammer groups, they have a lot of structural similarity. Note the text snippet "I'm writing this with tears in my eyes". This is a common scam message snippet that is not only used within the genre of stranded traveler scams. Text segments such as *with tears in my eyes* are useful phrases indicative of a scammer

of the content would not be helpful, as the scammers frequently rewrite messages, and—for high-value scams—by addressing the recipient by name.

As soon as the scammer realizes that his scam message is blocked, he will tweak it. And if that change is not enough to get it through, because the expected profit per email sent is much higher for this scam than for typical spam messages, the scammer could conceivably rewrite, or at least modify, the message for each transmission.

Despite the numerous differences between the emails in Figs. 7.1 and 7.2, which might allow them to evade a traditional email digest based filter, the two emails have numerous similarities. To begin with, both messages pretend to come from somebody the recipient knows. Without such a pretense, the emails are not likely to succeed. Second, both contain words associated with the supposed event. Consider using the following terms as "synonyms", where the words that were used in the above examples are underlined: {mugged, robbed, robbery, burglarized, stole, stolen, gunpoint, theft, thief, burglar}. Let's call these the *stranded traveler event words*. Both emails also contain *temporal words*: {as soon as, now, right away, immediately, COB, EOD, today, quickly, urgent, urgency}. These words are also common for emails of this genre. And both of them contain a *request*: {help, assist, assistance, send, loan, lend}. In addition, they both contain *stranded traveler scammer terms*, common words and phrases in the context of this type of scam: {London, Manila, vacation, trip, hotel, cell, money, cash, credit, tears in my eyes, Western Union, please, I beg you, passport, flight}. For sake of explanation, the sets described above are a bit shorter than the actual sets. The words and phrases comprising the sets can be extracted by an expert or by a person who has seen a sufficient number of these scam messages. Alternatively, extraction can be done via an automated method in which common phrases and their synonyms are identified and grouped.

What do we do with these phrases then? Say that we have a system that identifies a stranded traveler scam by scanning the content of an email and identifying which of the above sets are "satisfied". For simplicity, let's assume that the rule is [*stranded traveler event words* AND *request words* AND (*temporal words* OR *stranded traveler scammer terms*)]. Both of these emails would have triggered this rule. This is a storyline-based scam detector.

Now, let's look at a third example in the genre (Fig. 7.3) and see if it would also have been detected by the rule described above. First of all, are there any *stranded traveler event words*? Yes: "mugged", "robbery" and "stolen." Any request words? Yes: "loan" and "help". Temporal words? Yes: "ASAP". And how about stranded traveler scammer terms? Yes, *lots* of them: "London", "vacation", "hotel", "cash", "credit", "flight". As you can see, in spite of the different formulations, all these three emails trigger the same rule, based on a storyline of common elements. A meaningful scam countermeasure must be able to capture these common elements; an effective scam countermeasure must also avoid a large number of false positives. Let's consider an email that does not belong to the stranded traveler category—in fact, one that is not a scam at all.

---

**Subject: My Plight**

Im writing this message to you with sadness. I traveled to
London for a short vacation and unfortunately for me. I was
mugged at a knife point last night at the park of the hotel
where i lodged and all cash, credit cards and cell phone were
all stolen from me, I have reported the robbery to the police
but they are yet to find the muggers. My flight leaves in less
than 18hrs from now and i am having problems paying my hotel
bills. The hotel manager wont let me leave until i settle the
bills. Please, I need a loan from you to return back home and i
want you to get back to me ASAP if you can help.

---

**Fig. 7.3** Example 3, stranded traveler scam. This is a third example of a stranded traveler scam email. It has the same essential storyline as the other two examples, but uses different formulations

---

**Subject: vacation!!!**

Dear Joshua,
Having a great time in London. Saw the Tower of London and the
Changing of the Guard. Hoping to make it to Kew Gardens next.
I'll send photos!

Don't forget to water the plants. And could you pick us up next
week at the airport? I'll send the flight info.

Mom and Dad.

---

**Fig. 7.4** Example 4, a good email. This is an example email that is *not* a stranded traveler scam—in fact, it is not a scam at all. The storyline filter we describe will not trigger on this email

Only two of the categories—the *request* category ("send") and the *stranded traveler scammer terms* category ("London" and "flight") are triggered by the email in Fig. 7.4. There are no *stranded traveler event words* (such as "mugged") and no temporal words (such as "ASAP"). As a result, the rule described above is not triggered by this email. Of course, it is not quite that easy to conclude that the rule we described is good. After all, if the sender of the email in Fig. 7.4 had added "Today, Lucy stole a kiss from a stranger", it would have been misclassified, since "today" and "stole" correspond to temporal words and stranded traveler event words. In order to minimize false positives, one has to scan a very large number of legitimate emails and verify that they do not trigger the filter. If a filter causes too many false positives, one has to add additional limitations—in the rule (*stranded traveler event words* AND *request words* AND (*temporal words* OR *stranded traveler scammer terms*)), there are four of these, *event words* being the first and (*temporal words* OR *stranded traveler scammer terms*) being the fourth. By adding more and more, of course, the false negative rate will increase. It is a careful balancing act.

One benefit of the method described above is that it leads to an automatic classification of the emails. For example, the rule described above might be called *Stranded Traveler rule #6* (suggesting that there may be at least five other stranded traveler rules), whereas the rule (*email from a stranger* AND *expression of surprise words* AND *large sum of money words* AND *lottery words* AND *response words*) may correspond to a Lottery scam and the rule (*email from a stranger* AND *deceptive email address* AND *tax document term* AND *request works* and *temporal words*) describes one out of several rules to detect Business Email Compromise scams. The notion of "deceptive email address" will be described in Chap. 11.

## 7.3 Detecting Brand Abuse

A storyline filter can also be used to detect brand abuse. For example, consider Fig. 7.5. That has the exact format of a payment notification from PayPal. One can automatically determine that it matches this template using a method closely related to the storyline approach described above. For example, consider text segments such as "Transaction ID:", "Just thought you'd like to know", "Once the money's there you", "Get a PayPal Debit", "Don't see the money", "by an automated system, so", "at the bottom of any page", "PayPal is located at 2211". A message appearing to come from PayPal can easily be identified by the presence of some sufficient number of these.

Once an email is identified as appearing—to an end user—as being likely to be sent from PayPal, the next question is: Who *did* send it? Was it PayPal? If the sender is PayPal, then there should be a DMARC signature generated by PayPal. If this signature is valid, then the message is ok. If the message was *originally* sent by PayPal, and then forwarded from the original recipient to the current recipient (maybe the spouse of the original recipient) then the message is fine, too. This case corresponds to a sender who is trusted to the recipient. (See Chap. 11 for other uses of a trust assessment tool). The third case is that the message was neither sent by PayPal nor by a trusted party. This means that it is a potentially dangerous message, and should be filtered.

To avoid that an adversary reformulates the message without changing its meaning—e.g., by replacing "Just thought you'd like to know" with "We thought you would like to know"—there is a need for normalization of each text element, which can also be thought of as the use of equivalence classes.

This example shows that storyline detection can be used both to identify messages that correspond to well-known scams and to identify messages that either are from reputable senders—or which mimic such senders. This can be applied to bank statements, payment notifications, update requests from security service providers—you name it—any trusted brand that sends out notifications that can be mimicked by scammers. Without an understanding that the content appears to a human recipient as if it came from a trusted party, it may not be possible to know that the message is bad since the sender may not trigger any "traditional" spam filter rules.

**PayPal**

**Joe Schmoe sent you $18,000.00 USD**      Transaction ID: <u>4C154238G46983741</u>

Dear Alice Anderson,

Just thought you'd like to know Joe Schmoe sent you $18,000.00 USD.

**Note from Joe Schmoe:**

This is the payment for the car ($15,000). And $3000 for you to pay the shipper with.
Please remember that they can only accept cash, not checks or credit cards. They will call
you later today to set up a time to pick up the car.

Get the details

Once the money's there you can:

     Spend the money online at thousands of stores that accept PayPal.

     Transfer it to your bank account (takes 2-3 days).

     Get a PayPal Debit MasterCard.

**Don't see the money in your account?**

Don't worry - sometimes it just takes a few minutes for it to show up.

Sincerely,
PayPal

Help | Resolution Center | Security Center

This email was sent by an automated system, so if you reply, nobody will see it. To get in touch with us, log in to
your account and click "Contact Us" at the bottom of any page.

Copyright © 2016 PayPal, Inc. All rights reserved. PayPal is located at 2211 N. First St., San Jose, CA 95131.

**Fig. 7.5** Example of brand abuse. The figure shows an email appearing to be a PayPal payment
notification, suggesting that the email recipient received a payment. This is a very common
approach for scammers to trick their victims that they have been paid for goods or services. The
storyline tool, combined with sender analytics, can be used to detect such brand name abuse

# Part IV
# Understanding the Problem Starts with Measuring It

# Chapter 8
# Case Study: Sales Scams

**Abstract** This chapter focuses on a common type of consumer-facing scam referred to as the *sales scam*, focusing on the scam's occurrence on Craigslist, one of the most popular online market websites, with over 60 million monthly visitors in the U.S. alone. In spite of the prevalence of scams on Craigslist, the community's understanding of these is still very much lacking, and in this chapter and the two chapters following it, we present in-depth measurement studies of such scam activities. These measurement studies aim to better understand the underground economy of scams on Craigslist, and seek effective intervention points. In particular, we seek to address questions such "Where are scammers located?", "How do scam factories operate?", and "How effective are current defenses?". While the answers certainly do not translate to all types of scams—not even all those on Craigslist— they provide interesting insights into the problem and show how to design metrics to assess its nature.

## 8.1 The Automated Honeypot Ad System

For a quantitative analysis of scams, an automated data collection system was built to post honeypot ads, receive scam emails and interact with scammers through automated email conversation (see Fig. 8.1). The honeypot ads were posted on Craigslist and offered to sell a variety of goods. The system received and replied to and analyzed scam emails resulting from our advertisements. It also collected the IP addresses of scammers to explicitly confirm the geolocation of the scammers. Various analyses of the massively collected dataset were conducted to better understand how scammers work. In addition, observed scammer emails were clustered into groups based on a few key factors such as email addresses, shipping address, phone number and email payload.

### 8.1.1 Magnetic Honeypot Ads

Our aim was to create *magnetic honeypot* advertisements that would selectively attract scammers but not legitimate users. To do this, unattractive advertisements,

© Springer Science+Business Media New York 2016
M. Jakobsson (ed.), *Understanding Social Engineering Based Scams*,
DOI 10.1007/978-1-4939-6457-4_8

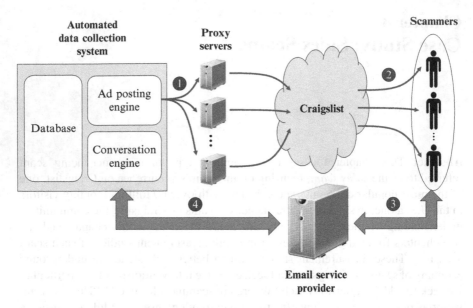

**Fig. 8.1** Automated scam data collection using magnetic honeypot ads. (*1*, *2*): the system posts "magnetic honeypot" ads that would appeal only to scammers; *(3)*: the scammers send scam emails in response to the magnetic honeypot ads; *(4)*: the system automatically engages in email conversations with scammers. Fraud attempt: the conversation eventually leads to a fraud attempt, where the scammer sends a fake PayPal notification or fake check, and urges the victim to send the goods to the scammer's mailing address

e.g., selling a used iPad at a price higher than new, were used. Legitimate users would not be interested in these items, but scammers do not seem to care one way or another. In fact, unrealistic expectations among potential victims is probably considered a desirable feature by scammers.

First, goods among a list of popular Amazon items were chosen to make sure that the our sales goods could be easily bought from Amazon or elsewhere. Then the selling price was set to be a little bit higher than the price on Amazon so that any sensible real buyer would not reply to such posts. Scammers, however, would; they might be using bots to crawl Craigslist or to automate the response process, or a lack of manpower might hamper the ability to carefully check the contents of each post.

### 8.1.2  Automated Communication with Scammers

An automated conversation engine was built to perform linguistic analysis of incoming emails from scammers and to automatically engage in multiple rounds of communication with scammers. The engine periodically checked inboxes of email accounts used for Craigslist accounts and downloaded all unread emails. Then it classified the emails to identify scam emails. The automated engine replied to a subset of the scam emails received—specifically, emails with a subject line that replies directly to the subject of our post. Subsequently, the automated engine exchanged multiple rounds of emails with the scammer, until the scammer made a fraud attempt, e.g., fake PayPal notifications or fake checks. The most common type of fraud we observed was a fake PayPal notification stating that funds had arrived at the victim's PayPal account and requesting shipment of the product to the scammer's mailing address. A typical example of email conversation is shown in Fig. 8.2.

## 8.2 Automated Scammer Interaction

We used our automated honeypot ad system to attract scammers and collect data on them during a period of roughly three months, from 4/15/2013 to 7/19/2013. Twenty locations including ten large and ten small cities/areas were selected from a list provided by Craigslist. The large cities included San Francisco, Seattle, New York, Boston, LA, San Diego, Portland, Washington DC, Chicago and Denver. The small cities/areas include Twin Tiers, Cumberland Valley, Meadville, Susanville, Siskiyou, Hanford-Corcoran, Santa Maria, Winchester, Southwest Colorado and Eastern Colorado.

Four product categories, cell phones, computers, jewelry and auto parts, were selected since they are used by many Craigslist users and therefore generated many daily ad postings. Our honeypot ads were posted in at very low rates, so that they accounted for an unnoticeable fraction of the total traffic volume in each city on Craigslist. Specifically, at most one ad per advertisement category was posted in each city every 48 h. The price of products used in the experiments ranged from $80 to $7000.

During the experiment, a total of 1376 magnetic honeypot advertisements were posted in our subject cities. Among all the advertisements posted, 747 advertisements were flagged by Craigslist, leaving 629 *effective* advertisements. Forty-two emails accounts (Craigslist accounts) were used during the experiment. The automated system was designed to post magnetic honeypot advertisements evenly distributed over posting time and product category to minimize possible biases in the collected dataset.

The average number of effective ads posted per hour was 26.2. The average number of effective ads posted per product category was 157.3. It is believed that the degree of variation observed in both distributions would not cause any significant bias in the collected dataset.

## iPhone 5 64GB (WashingtonDC)

**[from: cathy caraballo  <cathycaraballo93@gmail.com >]**
Still available for sell??
*[Our response]*
Yes, the product is still available. Please let me know if you
need more information.

**[from: cathy caraballo  <cathycaraballo93@gmail.com >]**
Thanks for getting back to me [words omitted] l will give you
$680 for the item in order to out bid other buyer and $60 for
shipping via a register mail down to my Son, kindly get back to
me with your PayPal email account so l can proceed now with
your payment and if you don't have an account with PayPal,
its pretty easy, safe and secured to open one. Just log on to
WWW.PayPal.com [words omitted]
Thanks and God Bless.

*[Our response]*
Sounds great. My paypal account is sarkadejan@gmail.com.
Thanks!

**[from: cathy caraballo  <cathycaraballo93@gmail.com >]**
Hello Friend.just want you to know that your payment has been
made paypal just mailed me now so check your inbox or spam and
your money has been deducted from my account pending to your
account.. [words omitted] tracking number and scanned receipt
for verify and Here is the Shipping Details below
[address omitted]

**Fake Paypal notification:**
**[from: service@paypal**
**<verifedtrackingshipp@mail2consultant.com  >]**
Dear Sarkadejan@gmail.com, You've received an instant payment
of $770.00 USD from Cathy Caraballo93, [words and images
omitted]

**Fig. 8.2** Example 419/PayPal scam thread. The first scam response usually has one or a couple
of simple sentences showing scammer's interest in the goods posted by the victim. The second
scam response contains a fraud attempt through fake PayPal or bogus check. The scammer's offer
is usually attractive since their offer price is higher than then victim's list price. Finally, the third
and later scam responses urge the victim to send the goods to the designated mailing address. The
researchers' messages were automatically generated using a conversation engine

## 8.3   Where Are the Scammers?

In this section we describe the results of our magnetic honeypot experiments. Our
collected data shed a great deal of light on the behavior of sales scammers.

**Table 8.1** Terminology

| Effective ads | Magnetic honeypot ads that are not flagged by Craigslist until the expiration (1 week) |
| --- | --- |
| Email thread | Several emails in the same conversation |
| First response received | The first email sent by the scammer to us after seeing our Craigslist ads |
| First reply sent | Our response to the first response received |
| Second response received, second reply sent | The scammer's response to our first reply; our reply to that in turn |

**Table 8.2** Summary of experimental results

| Overview | Duration of experiment | 97 days (4/15/2013–7/19/2013) |
| --- | --- | --- |
| | Cities/areas | 20 |
| | Product categories | 4 |
| Honeypot ads | Total number of ads | 1376 |
| | Effective ads | 629 |
| | Flagged ads | 747 |
| Emails | Emails received | 19, 204 |
| | Emails sent | 9902 |
| Email threads | First scammer responses received | 13, 215 |
| | First replies sent | 8048 |
| | Second scam-related response received | 1626 |
| | Fake PayPal payment emails (not threads) | 751 |
| | Bogus check payment threads | 885 |

## 8.3.1   Collected Emails and Threads

The total number of emails received during the experiment was 19, 204 and the number of emails sent was 9902. Several emails together in the same conversation are referred to as a *thread* (see Table 8.1 for a definition of "thread" and the other terms we use in this section.).

Among the total of 19, 204 emails received in our data collection, 15, 270 were first responses. Among these first responses, our filter determined that 13, 215 represented scam-related activities, while the remainder included spam, fake PayPal payment emails, and emails delivered from email service providers. As a result, our system attracted 9.6 scam trials (first scam responses) per ad (Table 8.2).

From the 13, 215 scam-related first responses, our automated data collection engine sent 8048 first replies. As mentioned in Sect. 8.1, presently replies were sent only to emails that directly replied to our posts. Of 13, 215 first responses, 9008 responses replied directly to the honeypot ads by including our ad's subject line.

For 1626 of the threads, the scammer made second responses. Finally, 751 fake PayPal payment notifications emails and 885 bogus check fraud attempts were received. Note that multiple fake PayPal payment emails (see Chap. 7 for an example) were received for some threads. However, it was not always possible to tie a PayPal notification back to an email conversation thread, since for most fake PayPal notifications the source email address is different from those used in the email conversation.

## 8.3.2   IP Addresses

In the experiment, 965 IP addresses were observed in over 22 countries. The total of 7759 accesses to the image hosting server were made from those IP addresses, and each IP address was observed eight times on average. Figure 8.3 illustrates the IP geolocation of scammers who have accessed the embedded image links more than once.

Scammers' IP addresses were observed from all over the world but most of them were located in Nigeria and the U.S. In particular, 50 % *of collected IP addresses were from Nigeria and* 38 % *were from the U.S.* Note that this figure is based on the number of unique IP addresses observed. It is also possible that some scammers could be using proxies, so the IP geolocation does not reflect their true location.

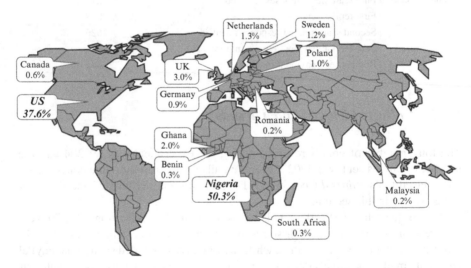

**Fig. 8.3** IP geolocation of scammers. For 965 IP addresses observed, 50 % are from Nigeria and 38 % are from the U.S. Whereas this is relative to the particular experiment described in this chapter, it matches to a large extent the general distribution of scam origination, although when it comes to malware distribution, there is a greater representation of former Soviet states (especially countries that end in "stan"), Brazil and Malaysia

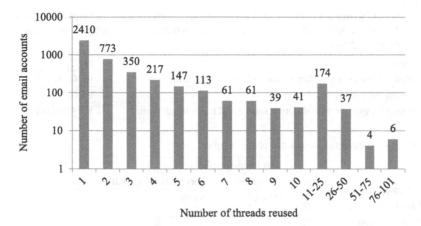

**Fig. 8.4** Distribution of scammer email account reuse count. Among all 4433 email accounts, 221 are used for more than ten threads, and one email account is used for 101 threads

### 8.3.3 Email Accounts

Throughout the experiment, scammers used 4433 email accounts for first responses of 13, 215 scam threads, indicating average reuse counts of three per email account. The most frequently reused email account appeared in 101 threads. Figure 8.4 shows the distribution of email reuse counts. Of the email accounts observed, 2410 (or 54 %) were used in only one thread and about 10 % were used in more than six threads. The majority of these single-use email addresses were initial inquiries about the product's availability that never resulted in further negotiations. However, many others were supporting emails used in the furtherance of the scam such as fake PayPal notifications, transportation agents, threats to contact the FBI (for when the product was not shipped) and similar emails.

For 82 % of the first responses received, the source email address was not the same as the reply-to address, and for 19 % of the second responses received, the source email address was not the same as the reply-to address. This source and reply-to address discrepancy is shown in Table 8.3. The percentage of discrepancy was much higher, 98 for first responses, within the top ten groups. The operating procedures of top tier organizations must account for the increased quantity of emails sent and received, both for management and security, which is why they were more apt to split source and reply-to accounts.

### 8.3.4 Shipping Addresses and Phone Numbers

One important attack attribution method used was shipping addresses. Throughout the study, 153 distinct shipping addresses were identified by threads that progressed

**Table 8.3**  Source and reply-to address discrepancy. Source address and reply-to address are different in more than 80 % of first responses, whereas the percentage is much lower for second responses

| | |
|---|---|
| First responses | 13,125 |
| First responses with different source and reply-to addresses | 10,826 (81.9 %) |
| Second responses | 1626 |
| Second responses with different source and reply-to addresses | 316 (19.4 %) |

**Table 8.4**  Shipping addresses and phone numbers

(a) Shipping addresses

| Location | # Addresses | % |
|---|---|---|
| Nigeria | 108 | 70 % |
| USA | 35 | 23 % |
| Other | 10 | 7 % |

(b) Phone numbers

| Location | Service type | Quantity |
|---|---|---|
| USA | VOIP | 107 |
| USA | Cellular | 80 |
| Nigeria | Unknown | 12 |
| Other country | Unknown | 3 |
| Unknown | Unknown | 4 |

Unknown locations are due to missing digits or area codes

far enough for expected shipment. As with IP addresses, the majority (70 %) of the shipping addresses were located in Nigeria with 23 % and 7 % located in the United States and other foreign countries respectively (Table 8.4a). Sometimes, two scams would use the same shipping addresses but with different recipient names, whether different aliases or different members of the same group. In one circumstance, seven names were associated with a single Nigerian address. For the classification of the threads into groups, emails with the same shipping address were assessed as belonging to the same group. Additionally, some addresses were in close proximity to each other. For example, three different apartment numbers for the same street address in Nigeria were used as shipping addresses. In these circumstances, the threads were not assessed as belonging to the same group since being neighbors did not definitively indicate the occupants were part of the same organization.

In some cases, scammers asked us to contact them via their phone numbers. A total of 206 distinct phone numbers were identified during the study (Table 8.4b). Most were given either as part of the initial inquiry or during the follow-on negotiation emails, with only a few numbers withheld until the end of the purchase and then provided along with the shipping address. Diverging from the pattern seen with IP addresses and shipping addresses, the majority of the phone numbers (91 %) were registered within the United States and relatively balanced, but slightly in favor of, voice over internet protocol (VOIP) over cellular numbers. Of the 15 phone numbers identified as registered outside the United States, 12 were Nigerian, and all of these were associated with completed scam attempts and aligned with distinct Nigerian shipping addresses. Four phone numbers were either missing digits or area codes and therefore could not be categorized.

### 8.3.5   Attribution: Performing Scammer Group Classification

To discover how prevalently these scammers/organizations infected Craigslist, and to determine the scope of their operations, the email messages were classified into groups based on similarities within their attributes. A very conservative clustering strategy was used to classify scam activities observed into scammer groups. Specifically, if two scam threads shared *exactly the same email addresses, shipping address, or phone numbers*, they were assigned to the same scammer group. Email addresses whose prefix were 90 % identical were manually reviewed along with other attributes such as email textual content and IP addresses, so series such as the biglanreXX@gmail.com addresses noted earlier were also grouped together when multiple attributes showed similarities. In this way, it is highly likely that two scam threads belong to the same scammer group when placed into the same cluster.

Based on this conservative classification strategy, an attack attribution was performed, in which it was found that *the top ten groups accounted for 48 % of all received scam threads* (see Fig. 8.5). Further analysis of the top ten groups showed that they operate over (almost) all cities where honeypot ads were posted, and most of them operated throughout the entire duration of our data collection (Table 8.5). Additionally, all groups responded to the honeypot ads from all categories of products: *cell phone, computer, jewelry* and *auto parts*.

Table 8.5 and Fig. 8.6 show group activities over time. As mentioned earlier, all top ten groups were active throughout the entire duration of the data collection. Figure 8.6 shows that peak activities of a subset of the top ten groups aligned with each other (e.g., the five plots on the left-hand side had aligned peaks and lulls.) Some of the top ten groups merged when slightly less conservative grouping criteria

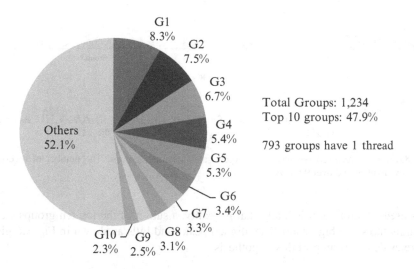

**Fig. 8.5** Scammer group by number of threads. Small number of groups account for about half of scam threads

**Table 8.5** The ten largest groups and the durations they were observed

| Group | First email | Last email | Duration |
|-------|-------------|------------|----------|
| 1 | 17 Apr 09:00 | 17 Jul 07:23 | 91 days |
| 2 | 17 Apr 23:12 | 17 Jul 14:03 | 91 days |
| 3 | 19 Apr 10:51 | 16 Jul 22:44 | 89 days |
| 4 | 16 Apr 08:37 | 8 Jul 21:11 | 84 days |
| 5 | 16 Apr 20:05 | 14 Jul 20:33 | 89 days |
| 6 | 22 Apr 12:58 | 16 Jul 22:09 | 86 days |
| 7 | 20 Apr 02:45 | 3 Jul 08:37 | 75 days |
| 8 | 16 Apr 18:07 | 11 Jul 11:15 | 86 days |
| 9 | 16 Apr 03:17 | 2 Jul 11:07 | 78 days |
| 10 | 17 Apr 15:04 | 14 Jul 18:21 | 89 days |

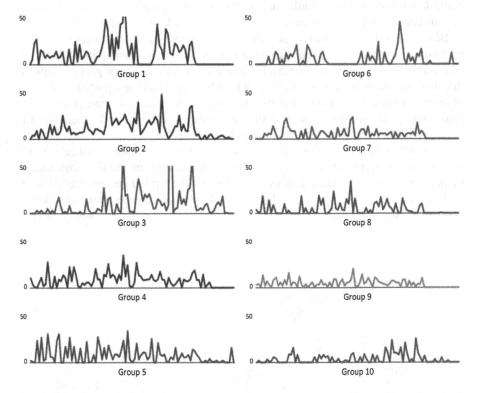

**Fig. 8.6** Emails received per day—ten largest sales scammer groups. The number of received emails were observed over 97 days

was used—therefore, it is likely that in reality, a subset of the top ten groups were actually the same big group. The aligned peaks and lulls as shown in Fig. 8.6 give more evidence to support this hypothesis.

## 8.4 Discussion

Our analysis reveals that these sales scams are highly prevalent, as honeypot advertisements on average received 9.6 scam replies. Perhaps the most interesting result of the analysis links *about 50% of the sales scam attempts observed on Craigslist to just ten groups of scammers.*. The ten most prolific scammer groups were sending targeted advertisements spread over many classes of goods and geographic regions of Craigslist. This type of attack attribution is important in guiding decisions related to which scammers to pursue. Attribution is also important for national security, as it allows the tracking of funds going to hostile countries and organizations.

Another finding is that 50% of the sales scammers IP addresses were located in Nigeria and 38% in the U.S. As we shall see, the geographical distribution of sales scam perpetrators is similar to the distribution of other types of scammers. The analysis of the message content indicates that message filtering could be improved by looking for combinations of patterns such as a reply-to address that does not match the sender's address, usage of uncommon phrases, and identifying and blacklisting of more stable and long-lived email accounts. Also, shipping addresses might be the starting point for law enforcement investigations. Along these same lines, the fact that only ten groups of scammers accounted for nearly half of the scams we received indicates that it might be possible to target and disrupt these groups, greatly reducing the prevalence of this scam.

# Chapter 9
# Case Study: Rental Scams

**Abstract** In this chapter, a systematic empirical study of the online rental scams on Craigslist and its ecosystem is presented. By developing several effective detection techniques, several major rental scam campaigns on Craigslist were identified. In addition, a system was built to automatically contact suspected rental scammers, which enabled us to understand what support infrastructure they used and how they were monetizing their postings.

We found that a diverse set of methods was utilized by scammers to monetize the rental scams. These included attempts to trick people into paying for credit reports and "bait-and-switch" rental listings. According to the investigation of rental scammers' payment method, five of the seven major scam campaigns identified used credit cards. Many campaigns also depended on businesses registered in the United States to collect payments. Another finding showed that Craigslist's filtering methods currently remove less than half of the rental scam ads we detected.

These experimental results highlight the fact that scammers are customizing their monetization methods to a great extent. Our study also uncovered new scams and infrastructure that were not encountered in previous studies [2–4]. This highlights the need to understand a wider range of scam domain and suggests potential bottlenecks for many scam monetizing strategies at the regulatory and payment layers. For instance, United States regulatory agencies such as the Federal Trade Commission (FTC) could investigate these companies and levy fines for their deceptive advertising practices. Another potential method of demonetizing these companies might be to alert credit card issuers, such as Visa or MasterCard, to these merchants' deceptive billing and refund policies.

## 9.1 Dataset

Throughout this chapter, a rental listing is defined as a scam if (1) it is fraudulently advertising a property that is not available or not lawfully owned by the advertiser and (2) it attempts to extract money from responders using either advanced fee fraud or "bait-and-switch" tactics.

© Springer Science+Business Media New York 2016

M. Jakobsson (ed.), *Understanding Social Engineering Based Scams*,
DOI 10.1007/978-1-4939-6457-4_9

This study relied upon repeated crawls of the rental section of Craigslist in different geographic locations to collect all listings posted in these regions and to flag those listing meeting our above definition of rental scam. Flagging was done using a combination of manual searching for reported rental scams and human-generated regular expressions. For a small subset of listings that were difficult to classify as being either scams or legitimate, an automated conversation engine was used to contact the poster to determine the validity of the listing. Finally, five other popular rental listing sites were crawled to detect cloned listings that had been re-posted to Craigslist, potentially by scammers.

## 9.1.1   Rental Listing Crawling

Our primary data set is based on listings collected from daily crawls of rental sections on Craigslist across the twenty cities and areas in the United States with the largest population [7]: New York, Los Angeles, Chicago, Houston, Philadelphia, San Antonio, San Diego, Dallas, San Francisco (Bay area), Austin, Jacksonville, Indianapolis, Columbus, Charlotte, Detroit, El Paso, Memphis, Boston and Seattle. Our crawler revisited each crawled ad 3 days after the first visit to detect if they had been flagged by Craigslist. The crawler performed a final recrawl of any unflagged listings 7 days after the first visit to determine if they had been flagged or had expired. Rental ads from five additional major rental listing websites, *Zillow, Trulia, Realtor.com, Yahoo! Homes* and *Homes.com* were also collected.

The crawler tracked all rental section ads for twenty cities/areas on Craigslist for a total duration of 141 days, from 2/24/2014 to 7/15/2014. Table 9.1 shows the overall summary of this dataset. In total, we collected over two million ads, of which 126,898 had been flagged by Craigslist.

**Table 9.1**  Dataset summary

|           |                    |                           |
|-----------|--------------------|---------------------------|
| Overview  | Duration           | 141 days (2/24/14–7/15/14) |
|           | Cities/areas       | 20                        |
| Rental ads | Total posted       | 2, 085, 663               |
|           | Flagged for removal | 126, 898  (6.1 %)         |
|           | Deleted (by user)  | 338, 362 (16.2 %)         |
|           | Expired            | 1, 620, 403 (77.7 %)      |

About 6 % of rental ads are flagged for removal by Craigslist. Rental ads are considered to be expired 7 days after being posted

## 9.1.2 Campaign Identification

The crawling of Craigslist produced a large set of flagged and non-flagged ads that were potentially scam listings. We knew that some of these ads were scams and that many were linked to a smaller number of distinct scam campaigns. Due to the large number of ads in our data set, a brute-force approach of manual analysis would have been ineffective and would have required a domain specific understanding of how scam ads differ from legitimate ads. Consequently, the knowledge of scam postings was bootstrapped by finding a small number of suspicious ads in a semi-automated manner. To this end, a broad range of user submitted scam reports online [1, 5, 6] were surveyed to gain some initial insights about rental scams. Based on these insights, the following heuristics were constructed to identify an initial set of suspicious rental listings:

- Detect suspicious cloned listings by correlating listings posted to Craigslist with other rental listing websites, in particular, cloned ads from other sites that exhibit a substantial price difference.
- Detect posts with similar contents across multiple cities, e.g., posts with the same phone numbers or email addresses.
- Focus on ads flagged by Craigslist, and manually identify suspicious scam listings. As we will report in detail later, not all flagged posts are scam listings; and conversely, not all scam posts were flagged by Craigslist
- Identify ads that are similar to user-reported scams.

## 9.1.3 Campaign Expansion Phase: Latitudinal

For some of the campaigns, we identified and hand labelled a small number of initial scam posts. Based on these we wanted to use automated and semi-automated methods to identify other similar listings that were part of the same campaigns. To this end, a human-generated scam signatures approach was used.

The first approach was to manually inspect the handful of ads identified as in the same campaign and to summarize a unique signature to identify that campaign. For example, one of the credit report scam campaigns had the following unique signatures: email accounts corresponding to the regular expression "[a-z]+[ ]@[ ]yahoo[ ](dot)[ ]com" and no other contact information included.

Then the signatures generated from the bootstrap dataset were applied to all crawled ads to identify additional ads belonging to the same campaign. As detailed in later sections, a combination of human and automated verification techniques was utilized to confirm that scam ads identified by these signatures were indeed scams.

### 9.1.4 Campaign Expansion Phase: Longitudinal

Next, we wanted to confirm as scam the suspicious listings identified in both the initial and the latitudinal identification phases. To this end, we built an automated conversation engine to converse with the suspected scammer, to see if the conversation would lead to a phase where the scammer requested payment from us.

The suspicious ads were manually inspected, and it was found that some of them were clearly scams, e.g., the ads with specific phone numbers that were reported as scams by many users. For others, while the ads appeared highly suspicious, it was not clear whether they were scams or more harmless spam postings by aggressive realtors or other rental service providers.

Therefore an automated conversation engine was used to (1) verify whether a suspicious ad was a scam and (2) collect additional data. More specifically, first a few suspicious ads were selected and the email conversations were performed manually. Legitimate users were fairly easily distinguished from malicious scammers during the email conversation. For example, clone ad scammers usually wanted to proceed with the rental process online since they claimed to be away from town for good purposes (e.g., serving in mission trip to Africa). From the preliminary conversations, a set of linguistic features (e.g., keywords such as "serving in mission" or rent application templates) and other types of features (e.g., embedded links to certain redirection servers) that distinguish rental scammers from other legitimate users were generated.

The automated conversation engine was used only for the emails selected based on a predefined set of features. During the email conversation, additional data such as email accounts, IP addresses, phone numbers, links and payment information from the scammers was collected. As in [4], the automated conversation engine embedded an external image link into the emails. Once a scammer clicked or loaded the link in any way, the link led the scammer to our private web server that logged the visitor's IP address. In this way, the IP addresses of the scammers were collected from two sources: email headers and access logs to the web server.

### 9.1.5 Campaign Summaries

A high-level summary of the major scam categories and campaigns identified is presented in Table 9.2. Each campaign is assigned a name based on either the name of the company that was monetizing the scam when known or a feature used to identify the listings in the campaign. Applying the campaign identification methods, seven distinct scam campaigns that account for approximately 32,000 individual ads were found. For each campaign, the table lists the monetization category of the scam, the raw number of listings associated with that campaign, the percentage of ads that were flagged by Craigslist, the number of cities where the scam listings were found and the payment method used.

**Table 9.2** Major rental scam campaigns identified

| Scam category | Campaign | # Ads | % Flagged | City | Payment |
|---|---|---|---|---|---|
| Credit report | CreditReport_Yahoo | 15, 184 | 33.0 % | 20 | Credit card |
| | CreditReport_Gmail | 5472 | 59.3 % | 9 | Credit card |
| Rent | Clone scam campaigns | 85 | 87.1 % | 17 | Wire transfer |
| Realtor service | American Standard Online | 3240 | 62.4 % | 19 | Credit card |
| | New Line Equity | 3230 | 43.3 % | 12 | Credit card |
| | Search Rent To Own | 1664 | 77.5 % | 17 | Credit card |
| Total | | 28, 875 | 45.2 % | | |

Rental scam campaigns of relatively large size in various rental scam types

## 9.2 Credit Report Rental Scams

In a typical credit report rental scam, a scammer posts a false rental ad for a property not owned by the scammer. When a victim user replies to the rental ad, the scammer asks the victim to obtain their credit score by clicking on a link included in the email. When the victim clicks the link, a scammer-operated redirection server redirects the victim to a credit score company and includes a referral ID. If the victim pays for the credit score service the scammer will be paid a commission by the credit score company through its affiliate program.[1]

### 9.2.1 Data Collection

Initial postings for each campaign were identified by manually examining the Craigslist-flagged ads, and correlating contact information and unique substrings included in the postings with user reports found on scam report sites [1, 5, 6]. In this manner, two major campaigns were identified, which we will refer to as *CreditReport_Yahoo* and *CreditReport_Gmail* respectively, due to their use of signature Yahoo and Gmail email addresses.

From the few examples found manually, the campaign dataset was expanded latitudinally via human-generated signatures. Using the human generated signatures, additional scam ads were identified from the same campaigns. Craigslist had failed to flag many of the scam ads we identified. Specifically, for CreditReport_Yahoo campaign, we found 15,184 scam ads of which 33 % were flagged for removal by Craigslist. We found 5471 scam ads posted by CreditReport_Gmail, of which 59 % were flagged. More details are provided in Table 9.2.

---

[1] According to the affiliate program of *Rental Verified*, which is used by one of the credit report campaigns we found, it pays up to $18 per customer (https://rentalverified.com/affiliates).

## 9.2.2 Dataset Sanity Check

The suspicious ads identified by the signatures were verified to be scams in two ways. First, a sanity check was performed by manually investigating 400 randomly selected suspicious ads, 200 from each campaign. A suspicious ad was considered as a scam if (1) it contained no additional contact information such as name, phone number, street address or URL, and (2) there existed same or similar ads with different email addresses in the identical campaign. Via manual inspection, only one false positive ad was found in the CreditReport_Yahoo campaign, and two in CreditReport_Gmail. The email addresses used in the false positive ads were also found in other suspicious ads, and actual realtors who used those email addresses were found. Second, among a total number of 20,256 credit report scam ads identified, 227 from the CreditReport_Yahoo and 89 from the CreditReport_Gmail campaigns were selected randomly, and emails were sent in response to the selected ads. Among the emails sent, 41 and 78 email responses were received, respectively.

## 9.2.3 Two-Scams-in-One

Interestingly, we found that the CreditReport_Yahoo campaign performed two types of scams serially. In their first email response, they attempted a credit report scam as described above. The scammers then sent an email to attempt a "fake phone verification", in which the scammer indicates that a victim's email had triggered a junk email filtering and the victim needed to verify his phone number to continue the rental process. (We note that junk email filter and phone verification is not connected in any way for traditional filters.) If a victim visited the URL included in the second email, she was redirected to a fake phone verification web page, as shown in Fig. 9.1. This site is a replica of the actual phone verification web page used by Craigslist.

The fake phone verification scam process is described as follows:

1. Once a victim enters her phone number for the verification, the scammer creates a new Craigslist account using the victim's phone number and triggers the true Craigslist phone verification process.
2. The victim receives a verification phone call or text message from Craigslist and then enters the received verification code in the scammer's replica phone verification web page.
3. The scammer then enters the verification code in the original Craigslist phone verification process with the result that the scammer now has a phone-verified Craigslist account.

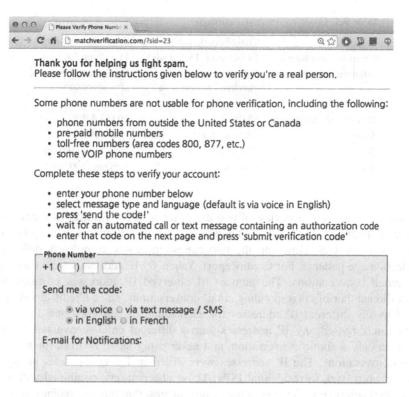

**Fig. 9.1** Fake phone verification scam. The web page shows the fake phone verification web page presented to victims. The victims unintentionally help the scammer get phone-verified Craigslist accounts

A scammer can monetize this second scam trial by selling the phone-verified Craigslist account for up to $5 on the underground market,[2] or he can use the account to post further rental scam advertisements on Craigslist.

## 9.2.4 In-Depth Analysis

Both credit report scam campaigns appeared to be located in the United States. In particular, the CreditReport_Gmail campaign appeared to be located in New York city, while evidence described later (e.g., diverse IP addresses and short inter-arrival times within bursts) suggests that the CreditReport_Yahoo campaign relied on a botnet for its operation.

---

[2]http://www.clpvashop.com/packages.html.

**Table 9.3** Credit report scam campaigns

|                       | CreditReport_Yahoo                    | CreditReport_Gmail                       |
|-----------------------|---------------------------------------|------------------------------------------|
| Email account found   | 14,545 from 15,187 ads                | 1133 from 5472 ads                       |
| Affiliated websites   | Rentalverified.com, matchverification.com | Freecreditnation.com, efreescore.com |
| IP addresses          | 69                                    | 30                                       |
| IP addresses used once| 65 (94.2 %)                           | 10 (33.3 %)                              |
| Country               | USA (100 %)                           | USA (100 %)                              |
| State                 | 28 states                             | New York (100 %)                         |
| ISP                   | Various                               | Verizon (100 %)                          |

Table 9.3 lists the overview of two credit report scam campaigns found during the experimental period. For both campaigns, all the IP addresses observed were located in the U.S. However, the two campaigns show completely different IP address usage patterns. For CreditReport_Yahoo, 69 IP addresses were found from 41 email conversations. The number of observed IP addresses is much larger than the number of corresponding email conversations, since CreditReport_Yahoo used mostly different IP addresses for each round of conversations. In addition, they rarely reused any IP addresses across different email conversations, using 94 % in only a single conversation, and never using an IP address for more than two conversations. The IP addresses were distributed over 24 states in the U.S. and mapped back to residential ISPs. These observations, combined with others described below (e.g., level of automation), suggest that this campaign was using a botnet for operation.

In the case of the CreditReport_Gmail campaign, 30 IP addresses were found from 78 email conversations. Of the 30 IP addresses, about 66 % were reused in more than one email conversations, and the maximum number of email threads that shared the same IP address was seven. All the observed IP addresses of the CreditReport_Gmail campaign were located in New York City, and mapped back to a single ISP, *Verizon Online LLC*.

## 9.3  Clone Scams

In clone scams, typically a scammer copies a legitimate rental ad from a different rental website, e.g., *realtor.com*. The cloned ad typically has the same street address and sometimes has the same description as the original ad. However, often the scammer lowers the rental price. This scam is typically monetized by the scammer requesting a money wire transfer or bank transfer for the first month's rent and a deposit.

### 9.3.1 Data Collection

To detect clone scams, our crawler tracked rental posts on Craigslist and five other major rental websites. We compared these ads and identified Craigslist rental ads cloned from other websites.

Overall, 22,852 cloned ads were identified spanning all 20 cities on Craigslist—however, not all of these were necessarily scam ads. The majority of these appeared to be legitimate users advertising their rentals on multiple websites. We then focused on the subset of 2675 cloned ads with a price difference of at least $300. These ads were deemed to be suspicious, but still it was not clear whether they are truly scam ads. To verify whether the identified suspicious ads were truly scams, 2517 emails were sent to suspicious ads using our automated conversation engines. From the emails sent, 237 responses were received and 85 of them were verified to be scams.

### 9.3.2 In-Depth Analysis of Confirmed Scams

A primary insight from our study is that most of these scams originate from Nigeria, and are likely operated by a small number of scam factories. To reach this conclusion, detailed analyses of the IP addresses, email addresses, wire transfer requests and bank account information contained in the scam attempts were conducted, as described in the following paragraphs.

Excluding IPs from well-known web mail providers, such as Gmail and Microsoft, a total of 89 unique IP addresses located in seven countries were observed. Of the collected IP addresses, 66 % were from Nigeria and 15 % were from the U.S. This is in similar to the result of the previous study by Park et al. [4] which showed 50 % and 37 % of IP addresses of Nigerian sales scammers were from Nigeria and the U.S., respectively. Even though we considered the possibility of proxies or anonymous networks, the consistent results from two studies strongly implied that the major number of the scammers were actually located in Nigeria.

From our conversations with clone ad posters, a total of 12 unique payment requests and eight duplicated requests for the same name or bank account were collected. Interestingly, the geographical distribution of payment request was significantly different from that of IPs, with 41 % of requests located in the US and 25 % located in Nigeria. For a money transfer via Western Union or MoneyGram, a sender needs to specify the receiver's location information including street address, city and country. However, due to the small sample size of payment requests it is unclear if any bias exists in the subset of conversations that resulted in a payment request versus those for which we were able to collect IP addresses.

A total of 22 distinct phone numbers were collected from 24 email threads, of which 64 % were phone numbers registered in the USA, half of which are identified as VoIP numbers. The rest (36 %) were registered in Nigeria.

**Table 9.4** Three largest clone rental scam groups identified by clustering on email address, phone number, bank account, IP address and application template

| Group | Ads (%) | Email accounts | Bank accounts | Phone numbers |
|-------|---------|----------------|---------------|---------------|
| 1 | 31 (36 %) | 21 | 4 | 9 |
| 2 | 16 (19 %) | 16 | 2 | 3 |
| 3 | 6 (7 %) | 6 | 0 | 2 |
| Others | 32 (38 %) | 29 | 5 | 8 |
| Total | 85 | 70 | 11 | 22 |

In order to better understand how scammers are organized and to perform attack attribution, the emails messages were clustered into groups based on similarities of their attributes. A conservative clustering strategy was used here. Two email threads were classified into the same group only if they shared one of the following: exactly the same email accounts, phone numbers, bank accounts, IP addresses or rent application templates. Since those attributes provide us with fairly explicit clues for clustering, we are highly confident of the clustering result. The result suggests that these clone scammers likely originated from *a small number of scam factories*. Through the clustering, a total of 15 scammer groups were found. Among them the top three groups accounted for 72 % of all observed email threads. More detailed information of the top three groups is illustrated in Table 9.4. While IP addresses of the second and third groups are largely located in Nigeria, those of the first group are spread over Nigeria, the US, Malaysia and Egypt.

## 9.4  Realtor Service Scams

Realtor service scams involve a special type of realtor service, such as *pre-foreclosure rental* or *rent-to-own rental*. This type of rental is attractive to renters, since they may eventually be able to own the property, while paying monthly rent similar to the usual monthly rent in the same area. Since similar legitimate services exist, we were very careful and conservative in identifying these scam campaigns. Realtor service scam campaigns usually request a victim to sign up for a private realtor service to get a list of rent-to-own rentals or pre-foreclosure rentals. To sign up for the service, the victim needs to pay up to $200 initial fee and/or $40 monthly fee.

While these businesses actually provide their customers with a list of homes, their rental ads are still considered scams since the ads are typically fake with unreasonably low rent prices, and/or are for properties they do not own. Moreover, many user scam reports claim that, in most cases, the properties in the provided list are not even for rent or sale at all. In addition, the refund process is extremely difficult, but this is not explained clearly before the customer signs up for their services.

### 9.4.1 Data Collection

As listed in Table 9.2, a total of 8134 realtor service scam ads were identified over all twenty cities of Craigslist, and about 57 % of the ads were flagged by Craigslist. Through the manual inspection on the crawled Craigslist rental ads, several phone numbers and URLs were observed frequently across multiple cities on Craigslist. Then the initial sets of phone numbers and URLs were extended by correlating them with various user scam reports [1, 5, 6]. Based on the human generated signatures of phone numbers and URLs, three large realtor services with advance fee campaigns were identified: *American Standard Online*, *New Line Equity* and *Search Rent To Own*.

Among the three campaigns found, two were identified by sets of phone numbers and the other campaign was identified by a set of URLs. For the soundness of the collected phone numbers, we manually called each number and confirmed a set of numbers actually belong to a same campaign. It was also confirmed that all phone numbers of a single campaign led us to the same automatic response system. Then we conversed with a representative over the phone and confirmed the business name of each campaign. Table 9.5 lists three large realtor services scam campaigns.

### 9.4.2 American Standard Online

American Standard Online (ASO) was identified based on a total of twenty phone numbers. The set of phone numbers were gathered through our suspicious phone number detection method and from many other sources such as *800notes.com*. Using the set of phone numbers, we found 3240 rental ads posted by ASO over 19 cities on Craigslist. Among them, 62 % were flagged for removal. Their ads offer rentals with much lower rent prices than other ads in the same area. However, a user is not able to get the information about the property from ASO representatives on the phone.

Because ASO is a registered company in the United States, we could find their record from *Better Business Bureau (BBB)*. The BBB website shows that the company ASO has a total of 302 customer complaints and the lowest possible

**Table 9.5** Realtor service with advance fee campaigns

|  | American Standard Online | New Line Equity | Search Rent To Own |
|---|---|---|---|
| Scam signatures | 20 phone numbers | 22 phone numbers | 5 URLs |
| Payment | Initial fee ($199) | Initial fee ($9.95), Monthly fee ($40.95) | Initial fee ($109.95), Monthly fee ($39.95) |
| BBB rating | F | Not found | Not found (C/F) |

The table shows the BBB ratings of the sibling websites

rating ('F'). The BBB record obviously suggests that doing business with ASO could be highly risky. It also means that the Federal Trade Commission (FTC) could potentially investigate this company and enforce fines or criminal penalties that would de-monetize this campaign.

According to many user scam reports, the scam process of ASO is as follows. If a victim calls the number to ask about the rental ad, ASO never answers their questions about the rental ads. Instead, ASO requests a payment of $199 for an initial fee to get an access to their pre-foreclosure (or rent-to-own) property database. Once the victim signs up for the service, ASO provides the victim with a property list. Due to the nature of the term "pre-foreclosure", it is usually uncertain that the properties in the list are actually in the status of pre-foreclosure, and most of them turn out not to be for rent or sale.

At the time of contract, ASO lures victims by guaranteeing 100 % refund after 90 days in case the customer is not satisfied. However, their actual refund policy requires a wait of at least 90 days from the contract and at least three denial letters from the owners of the properties in the provided list. It is obvious that getting the multiple denial letters is extremely difficult.

### 9.4.3   New Line Equity

New Line Equity (NLE) is another campaign that provides a special type of realtor service. NLE campaign was identified based on 22 phone numbers observed over 12 cities. Based on the set of phone numbers, a total of 3230 NLE rental scam ads were identified, and 43 % of them were flagged.

Many user reports claim that the scam process of NLE is quite similar to that of ASO. A victim calls the number found in a Craigslist rental ad, and NLE requests an initial fee $10 and monthly fee $40. Once the victim makes a payment, NLE provides him with a list of pre-foreclosure properties. In many cases, however, it turns out that most of the listed properties are not for rent or sale. We could not find a record of NLE from BBB, but there exists a record with a similar business name, *New Line of Equity* which has a BBB rating of 'D'. Many user reports complain about the difficulties in terminating the monthly fee payment.

### 9.4.4   Search Rent to Own

The Search Rent to Own (SRO) campaign was identified based on five URLs frequently observed over 17 cities on Craigslist. Among the five URLs, one was used as the main URL and the rest were redirection links to the main URL. Based on the set of URLs, 1664 SRO rental scam ads were found and 77 % of them were flagged by Craigslist. Like the other two campaigns, SRO posts false rental ads on Craigslist and ask the victims to sign up for their services with initial and monthly fees. The BBB record of this campaign did not exist, but the records of two sibling websites listed on the SRO website were found. The BBB rating of those two sibling websites were 'F' and 'C', which are poor ratings for legitimate businesses.

According to the user reports, SRO first lures a customer by offering 3-day free trial service. However, SRO does not fully explain that a $39.95 monthly fee will be charged automatically after the free trial. We found many customer complaints indicating that they were not notified upfront about the fact that monthly fee would be charged automatically after the free trial.

## 9.5 Flagged Ad Analysis

Currently, Craigslist relies on a flagging mechanism to filter out scam and spam ads. Our measurement study reveals that Craigslist currently flags only about 47 % of all the scam ads that we identified. Further, for a subset of the scams (specifically, clone scams) closely monitored, the median time till flagging (for the ads that do get flagged) is about 13 h—see Fig. 9.2. The figure also shows that roughly 60 % of clone scam ads remain active for more than 10 h, and 40 % remain active for more than 20 h.

For other scam categories, our data collection method did not allow us to obtain the time of flagging for two reasons. First, monitoring all ads on a per-hour basis would generate too much traffic, and our experiments were designed to keep our crawler's traffic volume low. Second, detecting these unknown scams required some

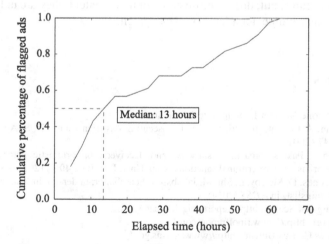

**Fig. 9.2** Time taken by Craigslist to flag clone scam ads. Our system monitored 85 clone scam ads and found that among the flagged ads, only 40 % were flagged within 10 h from ad posting time. In addition, about 60 % were flagged within a day

**Table 9.6** Classification of ads flagged by Craigslist

| Category | Campaigns | # Ads (%) |
|----------|-----------|-----------|
| Scams | Credit report scam | 8255(6.5 %) |
| | Clone scam | 74(0.1 %) |
| | Realtor service scam | 4572(3.6 %) |
| Spam | Local ads | 76, 752 (60.4 %) |
| | Credit repair ads | 2234(1.8 %) |
| | Legitimate rental ads | 10, 224(8.1 %) |
| Unidentified | | 24, 787 (19.5 %) |
| Total | | 126, 898 (−%) |

We determined that 10 % of adds flagged by Craigslist are scams, while 70 % are spam

manual effort. Hence, for some scam categories, we did not identify the scam ads soon enough to allow us to monitor them on an hourly basis.

Even though revisiting all ads on an hourly basis was too aggressive, all ads crawled were revisited twice—after 3 days and after 7 days—to determine whether they had been flagged. Table 9.6 presents a summary of the composition of the Craigslist-flagged ads. Of 126,898 Craigslist-flagged ads, about 10 % are verified to be *Scam* via automated email conversation. On the other hand, about 70 % are classified as *Spam* (as opposed to scam). These comprise local ads that are found usually within a single city and a few well-known, legitimate real estate companies. This leaves 24,787 (19 %) ads as *Unidentified* because we could not ascertain if the ads were benign or malicious. Some of these could be clone ads or other lower volume Rent scams, but, due to the diversity of their content, they are unlikely to be part of a higher volume, template-based campaign.

# References

1. 800Notes Phone Number Lookup. http://800notes.com/
2. J. Buchanan, A.J Grant, Investigating and prosecuting Nigerian fraud. U. S. Attorneys' Bull. **49**(6), 39–47 (2001)
3. C. Johnson, Fakers, breachers, slackers, and deceivers: opportunistic actors during the foreclosure crisis deserve criminal sanctions. Cap. Univ. Law Rev. **40**(4) (2012)
4. Y. Park, J. Jones, D. McCoy, E. Shi, M. Jakobsson, Scambaiter: understanding targeted Nigerian scams on Craigslist, in *NDSS* (2014)
5. Report Craigslist Scams. http://reportcraigslistscams.com/
6. Ripoff Report. http://www.ripoffreport.com/
7. United States Census Bureau. http://www.census.gov/

# Chapter 10
# Case Study: Romance Scams

**Abstract** This chapter describes the romance scam, and an experiment performed to establish metrics around it, including a data collection tool we refer to as the *simulated spam filter*. We find that while traditional romance scams still account for the large majority of romance scam messages, affiliate marketing scams are increasingly becoming dominant in online dating sites. This type of scam attempts to lure the victim to third-party sites, often promising profile pictures or, under the pretense of identity validation, phishing for the victim's credit card number. Our simulated spam filter study further shows that around 2 % of the scammers will click on links included in our auto-response emails, and that 5 % reply to our auto-response emails. Our results shed light on the extent to which romance scam operations are automated, and the approximate geographic location of the scammers.

## 10.1 Romance Scams: A Hurtful Crime

Romance scams are important to understand for several reasons. This scam generates the highest per-victim losses for consumer-facing scams—the IC3s 2014 report [1] pegs the average loss per reported instance at above $14,000, to be compared to slightly above $3000 for auto scams, a bit more than $1000 for Government Impersonation scams and just around $2000 for real estate scams. The scam also inflicts the greatest psychological impact on the victims. For example, a typical victim of a stranded traveler scam warns his friends of what happened. After all, he lost money trying to help a friend, after which his life more or less returns to normal. In contrast, interviews with victims of romance scams reveal that these victims commonly withdraw from their regular activities, especially those related to the Internet. They commonly feel a significant loss of trust and terrible embarrassment. Being asked the question "whom have you told?", most of the victims of romance scams respond "nobody". The sadness and the stigma make sharing difficult. The Romance scam is the most commonly reported scam for women in their 40s and 50s, according to the FBI/IC3. For women in their 50s, the losses exceed $27,000 on average, commonly significantly impacting their financial well-being.

© Springer Science+Business Media New York 2016

M. Jakobsson (ed.), *Understanding Social Engineering Based Scams*,
DOI 10.1007/978-1-4939-6457-4_10

From a technical perspective, romance scams differ from many other scams. While many scams require a very small number of victim-scammer interactions, romance scams commonly last for many months (with the noteworthy exception of what we call "hit-and-run" romance scams, described later in this chapter). The common long-term scams require the scammer to constantly receive emails, to generate sweet and inspiring responses, and to maintain the semblance of a real (online) relationship. At the same time, they must keep the labor costs as low as possible. This results in a need for large-scale cutting and pasting from pre-written scripts. Scammers perform minor customization to incorporate the location and name of the intended victim. Figure 10.1 shows two different romance scam messages, illustrating their great similarity. Note that the similarity is in segments, rendering traditional digest-based detection mechanisms fruitless. Romance scam scripts are bartered on underground forums, labelled by the ethnicity, age and gender of the intended victim. Whereas most other scams strictly follow predictable storylines, making them easy to detect using storyline-based filtering, (described in Chap. 7), romance scams do not. As with a conversation between two people who know each other reasonably well, they go in all directions, describing daydreams, mundane events, fears and wishes. To detect romance scams, it is helpful to identify long sequences of words that have been used in other, previous instances of romance scams. This is a bit similar to how traditional anti-virus detection mechanisms attempt to identify unusual sequences of bits, and capitalizes on the fact that romance scammers reuse text to a very large extent. This reuse is a financial necessity given the large quantities of interaction required to make traditional romance scams succeed.

Romance scams also stand out from a crime enabling perspective; many victims of romance scams are recruited to act as money mules. A money mule is a person who receives payments into his or her account, typically the proceeds of other scams, and performs payments or transfers using these funds. Romance victims commonly do this, believing that they are assisting the person, with whom they developed a relationship, with his or her (legitimate) business. Therefore, romance scam victims help scammers transfer profits, complicating tracking and blocking of the transfers by law enforcement. Consequently, identifying money mules is an important task.

In this chapter, we describe a study carried out on the personals section of Craigslist that identifies common methods of romance scammers, and we describe methods used for attack attribution. While Craigslist is an excellent place to study romance scams, it is far from the only place where these occurs. In fact, while different dating sites appear to be subject to the problem to various extents, we are not aware of any dating site that is immune to romance scams.

Hello

Hi,How are you doing over there.i don't know if you get this,well **i am to tell you little about me and also hope to know more about you before moving forward or exchanging #..Well i do stay here** in Douglas Ave SE, Auburn, WA *and i would really like to find out more about you ,but i don't always get online to chat but i always update my email account....***I believe in getting to know someone 1st that friendships are built. I believe in an open communication, being honest, and having integrity.** *Honoring and respecting each other is high on my list. I treat people the way i like to be treated and i believe what comes around goes around.* **I am a very compassionate person,** *I am in no rush, I think it's very important to take time to get to know someone, just has it has happened in most successful relationships today.*

**Am looking for a man that will be able to listen to me , communicate his feelings to me , make me laugh, respect me, support me in every way, love me and only me, make me smile, protect me when needed,constantly reactive, and treat me right. I do not have the time to meet others out in a public setting......**

I got some questions for you now...I do hope you answer them in your next mail...

What makes you the person you are today? How long have you been in this internet dating thing?Any luck yet? What are you looking for in a woman precisely? Will you ever love any woman unconditionally?

I have attached some pics for you...

Hope to read from you soon Nora

I hope this find you well wherever you are. I decided to write you now .**i am to tell you little about me and also hope to know more about you before moving forward or exchanging #, Well i do stay here** Auburn , *and i would really like to find out more about you ,but i don't always get on line to chat but i always update my private mail account,* **I believe in getting to know someone 1st that friendships are built. I believe in an open communication, being honest, and having integrity.** *Honoring and respecting each other is high on my list. I treat people the way I like to be treated. I believe what comes around goes around.* **I am a very compassionate person.** *I am in no rush, I think it's very important to take time to get to know someone, just has it has happened in most successful relationships today.*

**Am looking for a man that will be able to listen to me , communicate his feelings to me , make me laugh, respect me, support me in every way, love me and only me, make me smile, protect me when needed,constantly reactive, and treat me right. I do not have the time to meet others out in a public setting**

Feel free to write back anytime,to me i love a long conversation.Why Some say's I am a fool for seeking love...I say a fool is one who does not seek it but i will love to see the caring and kind man to prove this wrong for having more believe that real love and God fearing men are out there. My full name is Miranda Dareke.

Care to read back from you,
Miranda

**Fig. 10.1** Two romance scam messages exhibiting a great amount of text reuse. The scammer behind these two romance scam messages (sent to different apparent recipients) reused large amounts of text, probably using cut and paste from a template. This is very common for romance scams, due to the labor intensive situation the scammer is in. We added emphasis to highlight segments that were reused. It is possible to detect romance scam messages simply by detecting the reuse of significant amounts of text from previous messages that have been classified as romance scam messages. As an example, if a filter were to detect the three strings "also hope to know more about you before moving forward or exchanging", "but i don't always get online to chat but i always update my email account" and "someone first that friendships are built" in yet another email message, one can be fairly certain that this is another romance scam message. One could think of such as filter as a *copy-and-paste* detector

---

**Subject: Looking for hot wife**
```
Male 52 year old lookin for hot woman to marry. It is ok for u
to smoke and drink but u need to knwo how to cook. Massage me
for a good tim
```

---

**Fig. 10.2** Example 1—A "romantic" magnetic honeypot ad. We posted this advertisement on Craiglist with the intent of only obtaining responses from scammers, and not "real" users in search of a romantic opportunity

---

**Subject: 53 year old mal looking for a hot wife**
```
I am a 53 year old male and I want to find a hot lady to marry
u must be curvy and knwo how to cook and be nice in bed it is
ok if you smoke and drink Please email me and I will send u a
picture of my cars and me ok
```

---

**Fig. 10.3** Example 2—A "romantic" magnetic honeypot ad. This is another magnetic honeypot ad we posted on Craigslist. The goal was to get a lot of scammer responses but not to bother legitimate users. This ad performed very well, but we found that less outrageous advertisements both got fewer scammer responses, and in some cases, some responses from legitimate users

## 10.2   Collecting Intelligence

The methodology used in this study is closely related to that described in Sect. 8.1: we utilized magnetic honeypot advertisements (two of which are shown in Figs. 10.2 and 10.3) and posted them on Craigslist's "m4w" (men seeking women) forums. To avoid triggering responses from real users, we only posted ads to the 100 "slowest" cities in the U.S. on Craigslist—determined by the number of days that elapsed between the most recent 100 ads. This also helped our ads stay on the first page, which we found make them more likely to get responses from scammers. Twenty accounts were created for the purpose of this study, with each account posting to five cities. This was done to avoid throttling by Craigslist. Such throttling is used to curb abuse.

A new tool introduced in this study was a simulated spam filter tool. When we receive a message from an email address that has not previously corresponded with the recipient account, the simulated spam filter tool generates a message looking like an automated response from a spam filter. This message informs the sender that his or her email account needs to be registered with the spam filter service in order for the email to be delivered to the recipient, and that the only way to do this is to click on a link. The goal of doing this is both to test what percentage of scammers would click, and to gather the IP address (useful to identify the location of the scammer) and user-agent information (to understand the software and OS used) from those that did. In this process, we also uncovered scammer operations that appear to be automated.

**Table 10.1**  Categories of responses from our Craigslist personals ads

| Category | Number of messages | Percentage of messages (%) |
|---|---|---|
| Traditional romance scam | 314 | 58 |
| Affiliate scam | 107 | 20 |
| Phone scam | 84 | 16 |
| Other spam | 29 | 5 |
| Real responses | 8 | 1 |

## 10.3  Romance Scam Taxonomy

Over the 3 month period from April to July 2015, we received a total of 541 responses to our personals ads. Table 10.1 shows the breakdown of the message categories after manual labeling. We describe the major scam categories in this section.

### 10.3.1  Traditional Romance Scam

The vast majority (58 %) of the responses we received were traditional romance scams, where the scammers claim they are in a different state or country but want to build a serious long-term relationship. The messages commonly include picture attachments of attractive women scraped off other sites. This type of scam works by wooing the victim, sometimes for weeks or months, to earn their trust and then devising various excuses, e.g., surgery, travel, unexpected problems with work, etc., that require money or services from the victim. In our dataset, 60 % of the messages in this category originated from senders located in Africa, as determined by the timestamp and timezone in the SMTP header. This information is appended by the mail servers, and hence does not necessarily reflect the sender's timezone. Our observation matches that of previous work which showed that the majority of traditional romance scams originate in Western Africa.

### 10.3.2  Affiliate Marketing Scam

The second largest type of scam we observed, consisting of 20 % of the dataset, is affiliate marketing scam. In this case, the scammers' goal is to drive traffic to other Internet sites and to take a commission from doing so. Compared to traditional romance scams, affiliate scam messages do not contain elaborate stories about the sender's life and appear much better written, i.e., no misspellings.

To direct the victim to affiliate sites, the scammer commonly requests the victim to verify their age and identity on third-party sites, or to click on links for his or

---

**re: your post**
**[from: <lillypadlarson91@vfffmail.com>]**
Hi there again. Forgive me for not just running out to meet
with you, you are a complete to me at this point, though you
seem normal of course. Considering all things and scary stuff
that goes on in the world today, I'll be being cautious in the
beginning. So I'll need you to verify your age please. If not I
understand completely, If so great, here is the url. [removed]

---

**Fig. 10.4** Example of an affiliate scam message directing the victim to a third-party site

---

**Looking for hot wife**

**[from: Courtney <1e4ac0b3d37631fdb1a06e5047bc1f02@reply.craigslist.org>]C**
see the photo (attached), i will b here waiting 4 ur response.
am wanting 2 host u at my house, i'm in opeilka
and yeah, my address is: gineshumbleatgmail.com
*[Our response]*
hey hows it going?

**[from: Courtney <1e4ac0b3d37631fdb1a06e5047bc1f02@reply.craigslist.org>]**
really happy you answered. didn't tell you how old i am now
- am 23 i've checked, i can accom, you would need to get to
my house on oak park drive. which is in opelika if not, i'd
rather visit a motel... the motel 6 off i-85 seems nice. how
about you come and meet me at the village mall around 7? that'd
be good! it's fine if you cannot. let's talk more online now.
can't phone yet. i'm nervous! but click this here..... we can
talk there. http://benaughty.com/profiles/77v9/auburn9.html it
takes only 2 mins to get your profile, costs nothing too.

---

**Fig. 10.5** A customized affiliate scam message example

---

her "profile pictures." The affiliate site then asks the victim for his or her credit
card number to proceed. Figure 10.4 is an example of an affiliate scam message
requesting verification from the victim. If the victim enters his or her credit card
number, they are immediately charged for "monthly fees," sometimes from multiple
affiliate sites.

We also observed a group of sophisticated affiliate scammers that customized
their messages based on the victim's geolocation, which is likely determined by
the Craigslist city in which the ad was found. Specifically, the scammers asked the
victim to meet them at their home, a motel, or a shopping center/mall—all of which
are actual locations in the victim's city. Figure 10.5 shows an example of this type
of scam message, customized to a victim located in Auburn, AL. Figure 10.6 is
a screenshot of the site included in the scam message. Credit card information is
required to view profiles, despite the scammer's ploy to lure victims on to the site
by claiming that no fee is needed.

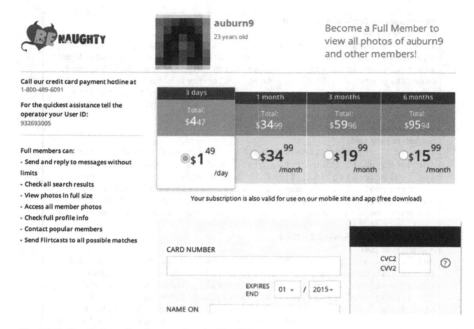

**Fig. 10.6** Screenshot of a site associated with affiliate scams

During our 4-month data collection period, we observed affiliate scammers modifying the contents of their messages frequently, particularly the initial response to our ads. Bigger updates to the messages were made every day or two, while smaller changes, such as a different phone number, were possibly made several times a day. Figure 10.7 shows how the text changed over 2 days in June, 2015. The first two messages are identical, except for the phone number, and were sent out hours apart, while the latter two messages were updated significantly and were observed about 12 h apart. All of the messages from this group of affiliate scammers appeared to have the same "tone", as if they were written by the same person.

### 10.3.3 Phone Scam

A third category of romance scam messages we observed are phone scams, comprising 16 % of our data set. The messages are typically short, e.g., "msg me here [phone number] if you want to chat with a real girl", though the phone numbers are different in each message. Some scammers intentionally obfuscate their phone number, possibly to evade blacklisting or to filter out responses from bots, see the example in Fig. 10.8. These scams often charge high pay-per-call rates, or will attempt to lure victims on to affiliate (e.g., dating) sites.

> **Sent timestamp 2015-06-07 09:28:00**
> **Subject: re cl post**
> This is a strange place with a lot of strange people wanting
> who knows what. Most of the posts don't even specify what they
> are truly looking for. I'd like a few dates, see what happens,
> chemistry etc.... I'm easy to get along with and very down to
> earth looking for someone similar. I really don't think it's
> too much to ask. Anyway, I have a pic. But people are more than
> their pics! you can text 12108122831
>
> **Sent timestamp: 2015-06-07 11:19:00**
> **Subject: re your post**
> This is a strange place with a lot of strange people wanting
> who knows what. Most of the posts don't even specify what they
> are truly looking for. I'd like a few dates, see what happens,
> chemistry etc.... I'm easy to get along with and very down to
> earth looking for someone similar. I really don't think it's
> too much to ask. Anyway, I have a pic. But people are more than
> their pics! texting is best 12319424270
>
> **Sent timestamp: 2015-06-07 22:27:00**
> **Subject: your post**
> Hello, how are you? Thought I would send a quick message and
> figure out how this place works. Not looking for anything
> really serious I guess, and don't really know that the whole
> ''online thing'' really works anyway but I thought I would
> give it a shot at least. I'm twenty five, down to earth, not a
> model but not too hard to look at. I work and take art classes
> on painting and drawing. I live alone, have a cat named Mr
> Buttons, 2 gold fish, and a number of plants. I like deep
> conversation, nature, people, butterflies, computer games and
> reading. I've had a few bad experiences dating but am willing
> to be open to a decent nice person. I don't have much and don't
> care what others have. I'm just me. lillymaylarson1990 at gmail
> dot com
>
> **Sent timestamp: 2015-06-08 18:55:00**
> **Subject: re cl post**
> Well, hey, just thought I would give this place a whirl and see
> what happens. I did try a couple of other places at one time
> with zero luck. I don't think it should be as difficult as it
> is, but then again maybe it's just me, dunno. A little about
> me, I'm 5, almost 26, bit of a geek, bookworm.....I love art
> and science, computer games, deep heavy conversation, dolphins
> and the ocean. I'm taking some art classes now and between that
> and working well I don't really have a lot of time. I guess my
> life is ok with just me and my cat but it would be nice to have
> someone else to hang out with and see what comes of it. I don't
> really have much myself so I don't judge people on where they
> are or what they have....who cares. Just be nice, that's my
> motto. I can send a photo if you wish to do the same, or if you
> don't for now I understand....I'll take a chance and send one
> though. lilly.maylarson.1990 at gmail dot com

**Fig. 10.7** Initial responses to our ads from affiliate scammers, and how the texts change over time. The first two messages shown here are identical, except for the phone number, and were sent on the same day to different supposed victims (that were all email honeypots of ours). The latter two message appear to have the same "tone"—as if they were written by the same person. However, the text goes through many more edits during the 12 h period

> **subject: craigslist engrossed**
> **[from: craigslist reply 9bb0 <9bb0575389b4387cac5a003af93d23ea@reply.craigslist.org>]**
> ```
> hello-- visiting the state your in!!! we should arrange
> something 347, six five six eight one zero seven txtme only if
> you're real
> ```

**Fig. 10.8** Example of a phone scam message with obfuscated telephone number

## 10.3.4 Simulated Spam Filter Results

As mentioned earlier in this chapter, one of the new tools introduced in this study is a simulated spam filter. For messages received from a newly observed sender (with whom the recipient had never conversed), the tool generates an auto-response requesting that the sender registers his or her email with the "spam filter" service in order for the message to be delivered to the recipient. The goal was to measure the percentage of scammers that would click on the registration link, and to gather IP address and user-agent information from those that did. In addition, this experiment also uncovered scam operations that appear to be automated; we received replies to the auto-response message that used canned text from a single template.

We activated the simulated spam filter for 2 months during June and July 2015 (the second half of our data collection period.) In total, our tool sent auto-responses to 297 recipients. Six recipients (2 %) clicked on the registration link, and 16 (5 %) sent email replies in response. One recipient both clicked and sent an email reply.

Of the six recipients that clicked on the registration link, three used IP addresses located in Africa (two in Nigeria, one in Cameroon), two used IP addresses in Canada, and one used an IP address in the U.S. Interestingly, one of the IPs located in Canada belongs to an Internet provider that offers dedicated servers and cloud hosting. It is likely that the scammer used the service to obfuscate his or her real location. All except one of the clicks were from the Windows operating system (Windows 7 or Windows 8), as determined by the HTTP user-agent string, with the remaining click from an Android phone. On average, the scammers clicked on the link 16 h after we sent the auto-response message.

We also studied the 16 recipients that sent an email response to our simulated spam filter auto-response. Eight (50 %) of those messages were almost identical, replacing only the email address or URL link embedded in the messages. Figure 10.9 shows an example of such a scripted response, which makes no reference to the previous message from the simulated spam filter tool. This indicates that the scam operation is automated—at least for the initial process of acquiring new victims.

---

**Registration Request**

```
This is an automated response. [our honeypot email] is using
SpamFreeToday.

Your email will be delivered as soon as you verify your email
address [link]. All it takes is one click, and all your emails
will be delivered automatically onwards.
```

**[from: Mel <ac7d7c1e55a933fdac29e64a8031e83e@reply.craigslist.org>]**
```
I'm doing great, nice to meet you babe. My name is Adriana,
36yo, no kids, how about you?

Let me say I really want to meet someone and have a good time,
but just as friends with benefits situation. I am too busy with
life to get into a real relationship right now which is why I
am here. So maybe something like hanging out once or twice a
week. I have only been looking on and off for about a week but
have not clicked with anyone yet. I normally like to be with
older guys but I would be up for someone younger if they know
what they are doing :p So that is my huge story lol so What
type of girl do you like? do you happen to want to live chat?
My email is acting really slow and I do not have kik and do not
text that much but I have a chat profile here [link removed]
Do you have face pics to trade? I added some pics, let me know
what you think hun :)
```

---

**Fig. 10.9** Scripted response from scammers that replied to our simulated spam filter tool. Notice that the scammer's message appears to come from a canned template, and makes no reference to the previous message from our simulated spam filter tool

## 10.4  Filtering Insights

It is worth noting how very few scammers were willing to click on the link in the simulated spam filter message. This suggests either that they are careful, recognizing that there is a tracking risk associated with clicking, or that they have such a large number of potential victims to pursue that the potential obstacle of a seemingly aggressive spam filter makes them decide to focus on other targets. This suggests clear benefit of deploying a real quarantine method to be used for high-risk messages, requiring senders of quarantined messages to click. Scammers would either decide to forego such opportunities, which protects the user, or risk giving out identifying information. Using a VPN helps shield their IP address, but still allows for the collection of identifying machine information. This, of course, is applicable not only to the blocking of romance scam messages, but any kind of scam. However, it is important to recognize that exceptions need to be made for senders that correspond to unattended mailboxes—such as newsletters, advertisements, and similar. Detecting such senders is relatively easy, though, based on their large volumes and recurring messaging campaigns, combined with heuristic methods to determine the owners of and age of the domains of the senders.

The affiliate scams had a very high "update frequency" for their first-round messages. They did not include their email address in this message, and hid behind Craigslist's pseudonymous user names. This makes it hard to algorithmically detect previously unseen messages, unless they share a sufficiently large text body in common with previous messages. However, our experiments showed that an automated conversation generator that responds to these messages will cause a second-round message to be sent by the attacker—and this one was much easier to identify. The reasons for this was both that the second-round messages changed much less frequently than the first-round messages, and that the email addresses included in the second-round messages (to move the conversation away from Craigslist) were long-lived. Given the extent to which the affiliate scammers contacted users who posted personals, it also will not take many honeypot personals to receive two identical messages for two very different geographic areas. This, too, is telling.

Traditional romance scams commonly involve the reuse of texts, as shown in Fig. 10.1. This means that by collecting a large number of romance scam texts (e.g., by scraping sites to which users submit scam messages, or using honeypots), one can build a collection of strings that are commonly reused. When these are detected in incoming messages, such messages can be classified as romance scams. Clearly, these strings must be sufficiently long (or unlikely) to avoid false positives. This would be a copy-and-paste detector. As new romance scam messages are collected, including by this automated detection method, shared strings would be extracted from these, adding to the reservoir of romance templates used by scammers. This forces scammers to reuse less in order to avoid detection, which in turn increases their labor costs or requires a greater degree of obfuscation.

A system that detects scam messages by the presence of strings must take into consideration the possibility that an observed message is a scam message, but one that is not sent by a scammer. More specifically, a scam message could be received by a first person, who forwards it to a second person, possibly asking for advice. The system should preferably not discard such messages, but simply mark them up with a warning and/or quarantine them and require the sender to click to verify his or her intention to send the message, as described above.

## Reference

1. Federal Bureau of Investigation, Internet Crime Complaint Center (IC3) annual reports. https://www.ic3.gov/media/annualreports.aspx

# Chapter 11
# Case Study: Business Email Compromise

**Abstract** This chapter looks at Business Email Compromise, first describing the structure of common aspects of this scam, and then turning to countermeasures. It is worth noting that many other scams have related structures—for example, scammers commonly use stolen accounts for both Business Email Compromise scams and for Stranded Traveler scams (discussed in Chap. 7.) Similarly, just as Business Email Compromise scams commonly use spoofing or masquerading using cousin-name domains, many Trojan Horse distribution campaigns masquerade as trusted senders to convince an intended victim to perform actions intended to infect his or her computer.

## 11.1 The Typical BEC Scam

Business Email Compromise scams—also referred to as "CEO scams"[1]—are targeted attacks that rely on an attacker's knowledge of trust relationships held by users in an attacked enterprise. In these scams, the would-be victim receives an email from what appears to be a colleague, a supplier or a client. The sender of the email, who is typically aware of the procedures followed in the targeted organization, makes a seemingly reasonable request, such as paying a late invoice or help processing a transfer needed for an imaginary acquisition of another company. The typically "business as usual" request does not contain references to any Libyan princesses, does not suggest the receiver has won the Internet lottery, and does not inform the recipient that he may be qualified to receive an unexpected inheritance.

---

[1]In one very common version of the BEC scam, a person able to perform payments and transfers in a company receives an email from the CEO of the company—or so it appears—in which the recipient is asked to help perform a transaction. In a version of this scam, also commonly figuring the CEO as the supposed sender of the scam email, a person in HR receives a request to transmit W-2 information about some employees. This information is commonly used to file tax returns on behalf of the employees, effectively allowing the scammer to steal money from the government by obtaining tax refunds on behalf of people they impersonate—whether these people really should expect a refund or not.

© Springer Science+Business Media New York 2016                                                115

M. Jakobsson (ed.), *Understanding Social Engineering Based Scams*,
DOI 10.1007/978-1-4939-6457-4_11

The recipient is not convinced using methods based on fear or greed, but rather, the attacker simply appeals to the recipient's wish to do his or her job well. What makes the request convincing is the reasonable context, along with the apparent identity of the sender of the email.

Making a request appear reasonable is a simple matter of obtaining and using information about the targeted organization or individual. Public information, infiltrated LinkedIn networks, and corrupted computer accounts from the targeted organizations, which are only *some* of the ways attackers use to gain knowledge of their intended victims, provide an easily accessed information base. Clearly, creating a reasonable-sounding business email is straightforward, and making it appear to come from a trusted party is *even easier*.

## 11.2   How Scammers Masquerade as Anybody They Want

There are three principal methods scammers use to masquerade as parties trusted by their intended victims:

1. The conceptually most straightforward method is simply to gain access to the email account of the trusted party—this is commonly referred to as Account Take-Over (or "ATO".)

   In a typical attack based on an ATO, the scammer phishes a first victim; call her Alice. Alice may, for example, receive an email stating that her email quota has been exceeded, and no further email can be received unless she logs in ("just click on the link") and requests a larger quota. As soon as Alice enters her user name and password, the scammer has access to her email. The scammer now searches the email, using the built-in "find" functionality, for words or phrases that indicate a relationship that may be of interest. This may be a word such as "invoice" or "CFO." The scammer may find several valuable relationships; assume one of these is with *Bob*, whose role, based on the emails the scammer finds, appears to be to receive and approve vendor invoices. The scammer now creates an email message for Bob and sends this from Alice's account, attaching an invoice with the same format that Alice has sent to Bob in the past, but with the banking information modified to correspond to an account the scammer controls. Bob receives the email and, assuming that the relationship with Alice is sufficiently trusted, requests for it to be paid.

   In an alternative attack, the scammer finds that Alice knows Cindy, who works for the same employer as Alice does. The scammer sends an email to Cindy from Alice, containing an attached powerpoint file and a brief message—"I was told to send this to you. Please review today or tomorrow. Thanks!" However, there is a catch: what appears to be a powerpoint presentation is a piece of malware. When Cindy opens it, her computer becomes infected—and now, the scammer has gained access to *Cindy's* email account as well.

2. Another way to masquerade as a trusted party is to spoof them. While spoofing is commonly blocked by DMARC [1], not all organizations support the DMARC standard. Spoofing is easy. The attacker just has to set up and operate a mail relay, and can then add any traffic that he wants to this, including fake traffic from Alice to Bob. When such emails are delivered to Bob, they will look legitimate to him, as if they came from Alice. In fact, if Bob were to respond to one of these spoofed emails, the scammer would *not* receive the response, but *Alice* would. For some scams, like the "infected powerpoint" attack described above, this does not matter much to the scammer, since the scam does not rely on several rounds of interaction. However, many scams do require multiple rounds of interaction, and the scammer really does want to receive potential responses. To address this, the scammer may add a reply-to address to the email he spoofs. Then, when Bob hits reply, the response will be sent to the scammer.

Not all email readers display reply-to addresses,[2] so Bob may not even realize that his response would be sent to somebody other than Alice. The scammer may then use a correct-looking *display name*. The display name is the name that is commonly displayed just in front of the email address. Anybody can set their display name any way they want to. If you want yours to be "PayPal", "Bank of America" or "Bill Gates", then you can change it right now. The attackers do. In some mail readers, the display name is the only sender information that gets displayed; the users never get to see the email address of the sender and reply-to addresses are hardly ever shown.

To further increase the odds that the would-be victim will not notice that his reply is not going where he expects, the scammer can create a look-alike email address and use that in the reply-to field. That way, the email that Bob composes will be addressed to a user that looks plausible, both in terms of the display name and the email address. For example, if Alice's email address is <AliceAnderson@organizationname.com>, then the scammer may create a free account <AliceAnderson@hotmail.com>, or register a domain "organizatonname.com" (notice the missing letter!) and then set up the account <AliceAnderson@organizatonname.com>. This belongs to the scammer now, but who would notice that it is not Alice? This type of attack is commonly referred to as a *cousin name attack*.

The scammer would then send an email to Bob, spoofed to appear to come from Alice, using the newly created account as the reply-to address. If Bob responds, the attacker will receive the response, and can then continue the conversation without any need to even spoof or use reply-to addresses; he simply writes back from this new account—the context of the email series will indicate to Bob that he is "still" speaking with Alice, in the unlikely event that he notices the address discrepancy later on.

---

[2]In fact, many email readers do not even display the *sender's address*—this is clearly a problem, as it simplifies the task of masquerading users dramatically.

3. The most common way to masquerade as somebody trusted is a simplification of
   the approach described above. As in the case of spoofing, we also assume that
   the scammer knows that Alice and Bob know each other. Social network sites
   like Facebook and LinkedIn makes it easy to find this information with very little
   effort, making targeting easy. The scammer then registers a deceptive domain
   name as above or creates a deceptive free email account. He is now in possession
   of <AliceAnderson@organizatonname.com> or maybe *AliceAnderson*123 at
   some free email service provider. Using this email account, the scammer emails
   Bob. Bob will receive an email from <AliceAnderson@organizatonname.com>.
   Unless the scammer is very unlucky, Bob will have no idea that this email is not
   from his trusted contact Alice, whose account of course is
   <AliceAnderson@organizationname.com>. This is the most common use of
   the cousin name attack.
       Notice that no spoofing was needed—which means that it does not matter
   whether Alice and Bob's organizations support DMARC. Moreover, the scammer also does not need to add a reply-to address: he is quite ok with Bob's
   responses going straight to <AliceAnderson@organizatonname.com>.
       This attack is difficult for users to spot, and traditional countermeasures also
   are not very effective against it. After all, what exactly makes
   <AliceAnderson@organizatonname.com> risky? It is not that this email
   account has sent millions of spam messages. It is not that it has a poor reputation
   (e.g., most recipients of email from the account place the email received in their
   spam folder.) In fact, on the surface, everything is fine. The *real* problem is that
   the account name is very similar—*deceptively* similar—to an account with which
   Bob has a trust relationship.
       It should be noted that the problem of deceptively chosen domains is not
   new, and they are used outside the realm of traditional fraud and for attacks
   related to phishing and Business Email Compromise. For example, a 2008 study
   [3] describes its used in political contexts, looking both at typo-squatting[3] and
   cousin-name attacks.

## 11.3   A Look at Which Senders Are Deceptive

What is deceptive to one person may not be deceptive to another. To begin with, if
you get an email from a stranger that appears to come from somebody you know,
that is a lot more deceptive than if you get an email from a stranger that looks like
it really came from a stranger. But of course, there are strangers who have names,

---

[3]In a typical typo-squatting attack, an attacker registers a domain with a reasonably common
misspelling, hoping that unfortunate users will make a mistake and either direct their browsers
or outgoing emails to a server controlled by the attacker. Typo-squatting is not yet a very common
approach among scammers, but is worth addressing, especially in the context of companies
associated with sending confidential information by email.

and email addresses, that look somewhat like people you know. When is an email address deceptive and when is it not? The best way to understand how to identify what is deceptive may be using a collection of examples.

- **Example 1:** Assume that you have a trust relationship with a person whose display name/email address is "Alice Anderson" *<alicea@zapfraud-inc.com>*, and you receive an email from a stranger with the display name/email address "Alice Anderson" *<alicea@zapfruad-inc.com>*. This is likely to be a cousin name attack—a scammer has registered the domain *zapfruad-inc.com* and is using it to masquerade as Alice. This is a high-risk email, and should probably be blocked.

- **Example 2:** Assume now that you have a trust relationship with a person whose display name/email address is "Alice Anderson" *<alicea@zfi.com>*, and you receive an email from a stranger with the display name/email address "Alice Anderson" *<alicea@zif.com>*. While this may look just like Example 1 above, it is not. The reason is that short ".com" domain names are precious, and few are left. An attacker cannot simply register *zif.com* in order to impersonate a user at *zfi.com*. This email should not be blocked.

- **Example 3:** Let's consider yet another example. You have a trust relationship with a person whose display name/email address is "Alice Anderson" *<alicea@zapfraud-inc.com>*, and you receive an email from a stranger with the display name "Alice Anderson"—and whose email address is
  *<alice1234@aol.com>*. What does this mean? Maybe it is the same person— Alice. You normally get an email from her work email address, but now, you get an email from her personal account. Or maybe it is from a scammer who has simply registered a free email account and set the display name to look like Alice's email account. It would not be reasonable for the system to block this email simply because of this similarity, but it may be safest to alert the recipient to the fact that this is not necessarily from the trusted person.

- **Example 4:** If we just twist the last example a bit, it means something else. Say that you receive an email from a stranger with display name/email address "Alice Anderson" *<alicea@zapfraud-inc.com>*, and you receive an email from a stranger with the display name is "Alice Anderson"—and whose email address is *<bobb@zapfraud-inc.com>*. Now what does that mean? It *probably* means that a scammer has corrupted Bob's account and changed his display name to read "Alice Anderson"; it *certainly* does not mean that Alice decided to keep her name but change her username to *bobb*. This is a dangerous email.

One way to quantify deceptiveness is to compare email addresses using a string-matching algorithm. For example, one can compute the Levenshtein distance between two different strings or use an algorithm such as Jaro-Winkler [2] to determine the distance. Using this approach, two domains (such as the legitimate zapfraud-inc and a cousin-name version called zapfruad-inc) can be compared. One can also compare two display names, two user names, or two entire strings of display and user names. A fair number of rules must be implemented, though, to capture all cases. For example, consider a trusted party with an email address *<alicea@zapfraud-inc.com>*—and then a stranger with the address *<alicea@zapfraud-inc.net>*. Is the stranger to be trusted? This may depend on who registered the two domains; if it is the same party, then the stranger is probably to be trusted, otherwise not. If whois[4] information is available for one, but not the other, then that is a red flag. If there is no whois information for either, but the stranger domain was registered in the last hour while the other domain is very old ... that spells danger. As you see, it is neither straightforward nor impossible to make a meaningful assessment of how deceptive an email address is.

We are now ready to talk about how to detect potential masquerade attempts, and what to do when these are detected.

## 11.4   Defending Against Business Email Compromise

Typical messages used by scammers launching Business Email Compromise (BEC) scams are sent in small quantities and from accounts that do not have bad reputation. The messages typically do not contain keywords unique to BEC scams; instead, the messages attempt to be as commonplace as is possible. Consequently, as explained in Chap. 5, BEC scams are not detected by spam filters and other traditional filtering technologies. Recipients are also not good at detecting these scams. But all hope is not lost. Let's talk about how BEC scam messages *can* be detected and blocked.

The first insight is that the best action to take depends on the type of BEC scam it appears to be. Let's therefore consider the three types of attacks described in the last section, one by one.

The most common attack, the cousin name attack, is characterized by a user receiving an email from a sender that is not a trusted contact, but whose display name, email address or domain look deceptively similar to those of a trusted contact of the recipient. The latter can be determined using string matching algorithms, where each pair of strings (such as "John Dougherty" and "Jon Dogerthy") are compared and given a similarity score. The similarity score tracks how *visually similar* two strings are. It also tracks how *conceptually* similar they are, giving a high score to the pair "Doe, Bill", "William Doe" in spite of the fact that these two strings are very different when considered letter by letter.

If an incoming email is from a sender that is deceptively similar to a trusted sender, but the account is not that of the trusted sender, then an action is taken. If the similarity score is extremely high, the email may simply be discarded; whereas if the score is moderately high, then the email may be marked up with a warning such as "This email looks like it comes from somebody you know but it is not from the regular address of that person. Be careful! This may be an impersonator. Verify the identity of the sender if you can, and do not send any valuable information or any money without making sure that the message is legitimate."

---

[4]https://whois.icann.org/en.

Let's consider now an email that to the system appears to have been sent by a trusted sender (say, Alice) but where the email has a reply-to address that is different from the sender's address. Let's further assume that this reply-to address has not been seen previously by the system, or at the very least, has not been used in a message that was deemed safe to deliver to the current recipient—say, Bob. This corresponds to a message that might be spoofed; however, it could *also* be legitimate, sent from a trusted sender who simply added a reply-to address to the message.

The system can place such a message in quarantine and then automatically generate a response to the email, sent to the apparent sender—not to the reply-to address: "This is an auto-response. Did you just send a message to Alice, with the subject line 'Let's talk'? If you did, please click here to have the message delivered to Alice. If you did not send this message, no action is required."

If the email was spoofed, the attacker will not receive the automated response, and therefore, will not be able to click on the link (which, of course, will contain a personalized, unique, and unpredictable string.) So the spoofed message will sit and rot in quarantine for a while, and will then get erased when it has overstayed its welcome. Most legitimate emails, on the other hand, will get delivered—except, of course, in situations where the sender does not notice the automated response. (We note that *most* emails will not get this treatment; only emails that appear to the receiving system to have been spoofed will be handled so. So most senders will not have to worry much about getting automated responses of the type we describe.) Finally, unattended email sending accounts can be configured to generate the correct response handshake, but only when the account indeed did send the initial message.

The hardest case to deal with is the one we have saved for last: detecting and reacting to an email sent from a compromised ("ATOed") account. First of all, since such an email really comes from the legitimate account, the headers may not carry any clue at all. The determination that an email is associated with an ATO risk is therefore based on the message content. If the content matches known BEC pitches or uses high-risk keywords ("wire", "account" or "invoice" for example) then it may be placed in quarantine. However, the system cannot send an automated response to the sender, asking to react to have the message delivered. The reason is simple; not only will a legitimate sender be able to respond, but an attacker will as well. However, if the system has a secondary channel for the sender—such as another email account associated with that person or a phone number to which an SMS can be sent—then an automated response like the one described above can be sent using such a channel.

If the system does not have a secondary channel associated with the sender, then an alternative approach is to deliver the message with a warning. "This message is associated with high risk. If the sender requests funds or sensitive information, then call or SMS the sender to confirm that the message is legitimate."

Using the approach described above, BEC success rates can be dramatically reduced by a careful combination of risk classification and an action that is tied to the classification. Like all other security technologies, of course, the approach is not bullet proof; on the other hand, it represents a large step forward—a step that is possible based on an understanding the constraints and methods of the scammers. As such, it is a perfect illustration of the beliefs held by the authors of this book: *We can make progress in the fight against undesirable behavior by understanding the exact nature of the problem.*

# References

1. Domain-based message authentication, reporting, and conformance (DMARC) (2015), https://tools.ietf.org/html/rfc7489. Accessed 17 Apr 2016
2. Jaro-Winkler, https://xlinux.nist.gov/dads//HTML/jaroWinkler.html
3. C. Soghoian, O. Friedrichs, M. Jakobsson, The threat of political phishing, in *International Symposium on Human Aspects of Information Security & Assurance (HAISA 2008)*, Port Elizabeth (2008)

# Part V
# Conclusion

# Chapter 12
# Conclusion and Next Steps

Scam developments and scam countermeasures are both in constant flux, with one reacting to the other. As scammers identify a new human or technical weakness, they change their techniques. This, in turn, refocuses the efforts of scam researchers and practitioners, and drives entrepreneurs to identify new techniques to provide protection. Scammers, in turn, temporarily retreat, try new methods, and modify and augment their approaches. This is not going to end.

However, currently, there is another dynamic to be observed: scams are increasing. Ten years ago, email-based social engineering was almost exclusively rather predictable-looking phishing attacks or the ludicrous attempts by Nigerian scammers. Only the most gullible were at serious risk. This has changed. Scams are now aimed not only at the most gullible, and are commonly targeted, making them even more credible to their intended victims. The early successes of a first generation of scammers has led to their numbers multiplying. Social engineering artists are now learning to distribute malware, and malware authors are learning new social engineering tricks to increase their infection rates. The increasing number of people making a living as scammers—or improving the lives of their families by moonlighting as scammers—is the problem. We are unlikely to *stop* scams, but we must aim to reduce their numbers, their impact and the profits reaped from them. Every dollar lost to scammers is a dollar invested—by the scammers—into more scams.

Many experts argue that scammers are stupid and their attempts feeble. While most of the scammers are still careless and hurried, making their attempts at fraud reasonably easy for careful people to spot, some are both cunning and careful. And it only takes a simple mistake for a serious loss to be incurred. Just as individual users do themselves no favor by thinking that they cannot fall for a scam, scam researchers and practitioners must avoid thinking that others are as vigilant as they are—or think they are. If you are a security researcher (or live with one), it is not

© Springer Science+Business Media New York 2016

M. Jakobsson (ed.), *Understanding Social Engineering Based Scams*,
DOI 10.1007/978-1-4939-6457-4_12

strange for you to be interested in how Internet abuse works and to keenly keep up with developments. But it *is* strange for the general public to be interested. They want to go about living their lives—not learn about the new type of Internet threat.

Moreover, there is absolutely no reason to believe that the scammers are dumb. It is much more reasonable to recognize that they can get away with doing dumb things, at least most of the time, while making handsome profits. We may be justified if we call them sloppy, but being sloppy is not an obstacle to success at this point. In other words, the *scammers* are not stupid. Often, the *countermeasures* are stupid; many security measures are afterthoughts. The Internet was built to be an open network. It was built without strong authentication. Spam filters were developed to block spam, but are now expected to also block scams. But spam and scam have very different characteristics. Many security measures can be thought of as road blocks in a parking lot: very easy to drive around.

The best way to develop and deploy ways to identify and measure the problem and how it changes is to identify not only what the scammers do, but also *why*. By understanding why, we can hope to develop countermeasures that are not simple patches that will only hold back the scammers for a few weeks. By understanding why the scammers do what they do, we can hope to design technical solutions, improved policies and better educational methods that address the nature of the problem. Understanding why the scammers do what they do, we must also understand their intended victims, what they do—and fail to do. We must attempt to look into the future, and determine what comes next.

We believe that it is important for the security community to study and improve their understanding of the following areas:

- The shift toward low-volume, targeted scams makes it important to design new security measures able to detect such attacks, where detection can be based on the structure of the headers, the content, or the reaction of the recipients. If attack instances can be clustered, this allows detection of anomalous patterns, including the response of recipients. Did any of them report an email as being risky?
- The integration of social engineering methods with malware distribution makes it important to consider the actions performed on a computer (such as the running of a javascript routine) in the light of the origin of the URL associated with the javascript. For example, was it an email from a stranger with a name similar to a trusted party?
- Scammers are known to re-use material that works. This is a labor-saving effort from their perspective, but can also be used to identify scams by automatically identifying emails with at least one "reused" scam text segment. When such emails are detected, it is safe to assume that they do not contain just one reused scam segment, but many. Automatically extracting these and putting them to use to identify other scam messages is important. An effective algorithm to detect text reuse could put a sizeable dent into some scam efforts, such as romance

scams, which are very heavily based on text reuse. Making romance scams more difficult to perpetrate would also help address the monetization of other scams, as romance scam victims are commonly used as money mules.

- An improved ability to attribute attacks would both help identify patterns and to focus the efforts of law enforcement where it matters the most.

- Understanding the "human aspect" of scams—whether on the side of the attacker or victim—offers the opportunity to identify likely trends before they start, and to address problems proactively. It also allows *appropriate* countermeasures to be developed, as one can test potential countermeasures with a user interface component before deploying them, to gain assurance that the methods will work as expected.

- An integration of scam filters and scam honeypots (such as those described in previous chapters) would help collect intelligence in a timely manner. Using large portion of identified scam messages to initiate automated conversations with the scammers would be a good start. What other ways are there for us to reuse what one countermeasure produces for the purposes of improving another countermeasure?

- Last but not least, we must recognize online scams as a serious threat, and focus our efforts accordingly. We must increase collaboration between service providers, technology organizations and academia through industry organizations such as the Anti-Phishing Working Group (APWG). We must create a bridge between government—such as the FBI, IRS and IC3—and organizations with data and insights.

We hope that this book will provide examples of this process, and inspiration on how to reduce the profitability of online crimes. We hope that by reducing the benefits of scams—and by increasing the cost, risks and difficulties scammers face—we can make old scammers retire and would-be scammers pick other trades.

# Index

© Springer Science+Business Media New York 2016
M. Jakobsson (ed.), *Understanding Social Engineering Based Scams*,
DOI 10.1007/978-1-4939-6457-4

Printed in the United States
By Bookmasters